When I Was Your Age, We Didn't Even HAVE Church

When I Was Your Age, We Didn't Even HAVE Church

Chronicles of a Catholic Parent

Kevin Cowherd

Illustrations by Jack Desrocher

Our Sunday Visitor Publishing Division
Our Sunday Visitor, Inc.
Huntington, Indiana 46750

International Standard Book Number: 0-87973-672-0
Library of Congress Catalog Card Number: 95-68833

Cover design by Rebecca J. Heaston

PRINTED IN THE UNITED STATES OF AMERICA

To Mom, the best Catholic parent I know.

Contents

Acknowledgments / 9

Introduction: On the front lines of Catholic parenthood / 11

PART 1
ROLE MODEL / MARTYR

You kids today, you don't know how lucky you are / 16

A bedtime chronicle / 20

First Communion and photo opportunities / 24

It's all over but the crying / 28

The no-work zone / 32

Quality time? In a pig's eye! / 36

PART 2
THE FAMILY THAT PRAYS TOGETHER

Your guide to saner worshiping / 42

All together now — uh, except for you / 46

Mr. Big Spender / 50

Peace be with me / 53

PART 3
TOO MUCH TOGETHERNESS

It's only a game / 60

The vegetable dilemma: Don't worry, be happy / 64

Say amen; say good-night / 68

No blood? It's a great party / 72

Eating out: The clock is ticking / 76

Having a great time — wish you were here / 80

PART 4
SISTER SAYS: THESE ARE THE HAPPIEST DAYS OF YOUR LIFE

What's wrong with this picture? / 86

Keep telling yourself: It's only a dream / 90

It's a small world after all / 94

Words to live by / 97

PART 5
COPING WITHOUT THERAPY: THE EARLY YEARS

Here's a shot of Timmy with our dog Zeth . . . Timmy's the one on
the right, of course. . . / 104

It's a dirty job, but somebody has to do it / 107

Three years old: It doesn't get any better than this / 111

Impressionism vs. post-modernism: Is it a tree or Baby Jesus? / 115

Honesty is the best . . . never mind / 119

It beats a spike through your cheek / 123

PART 6
HOLIDAYS AND HOLY DAZE

Way beyond cool / 130

Don't make me do it / 133

More than a man can stand / 136

Midnight Mass madness / 140

Acknowledgments

Acknowledgments. I know, I know . . . who cares? The reader thinks: Is this gonna be like the Academy Awards, where they get all weepy and go on and on about everyone who ever touched their lives, from their seventh-grade shop teacher to the facilitator in their support group who also sets up the folding chairs every Thursday night?

No, we'll keep this short and sweet. Besides, I don't even belong to a support group.

Thanks to my wife and best friend, Nancy, who'd support me even if I came home one day said: "Y'know, I'm thinking of rewriting the Bible . . ." Thanks to the best kids in all the world: Sean, Chrissie, and Jamie, who inspire me endlessly and taught me what real love is all about.

Thanks to my mom, Noreen Cowherd, for obvious reasons. You talk about a shoo-in for the Catholic Parent Hall of Fame.

Thanks to my sister, Maura Rose, and my brother, Steve Cowherd, and their families for their encouragement, and to my mother-in-law, Dorothy Phelan, to Beth and Doug Diesu and their family, and to Susan Scully, for the same reason.

Thanks to Greg Erlandson of Our Sunday Visitor for his vision of what this book could be. Greg looked at a middle-aged newspaper columnist with a just-out-of-Attica look to him and somehow thought: "Maybe he could write something for us that isn't *too* bad . . ."

Thanks to Woodeene Koenig-Bricker of Our Sunday Visitor's *Catholic Parent* for all her support, and for giving me my start in the field of Catholic humor. (There is a field of Catholic humor, isn't there?)

Thanks also to Jackie Lindsey and Henry O'Brien of Our Sunday Visitor for their patience and help, invaluable for a fumbling first-time author.

Thanks to Bob Bonney, who was like a father to me and is laughing his head off right now in heaven. Yeah, Bones, I wrote a book. Isn't that something?

Finally, thanks to Rob Hiaasen of the *Baltimore Sun* who, when first informed of the title of this book, looked up from his word processor and said: "Yeah, yeah. You wanna grab some lunch?"

That's a good friend, that is.

Introduction: On the front lines of Catholic parenthood

We should probably get my credentials out of the way first. For the first fourteen years of my life, I ate fish sticks on Friday. I had fish sticks for lunch in school and then I'd go home and ask my mom what was for dinner and she'd say: "I was thinking about fish sticks!" in a tone of voice that suggested we were going to try something new and exciting, instead of the same ho-hum meal.

Okay, let's do the math. If an average serving is five fish sticks, and I had two average servings each Friday and this went on for fourteen years, I ate somewhere in the neighborhood of — let's see, four fives are twenty, carry the two — 7,280 fish sticks.

Then one day the Church said: "You know what? A bunch of us were sitting around the Vatican and one of the cardinals, I forget which one, said . . . well, never mind what he said. The point is, you can eat meat on Fridays from now on."

Maybe the corporate bigwigs at Mrs. Paul's were sobbing and passing around the Kleenex after that announcement, I don't know. But that kid you saw turning cartwheels in the street? That was me.

Total fish stick consumption is all well and good, of course, but you need more on your résumé to write a book like this. And I have it.

I spent seven years in Catholic school wearing a snazzy white shirt, navy tie, and gray pants, my mind molded by a succession of nuns and Jesuit priests who convinced me that I was a pinhead one moment, and the smartest and most blessed boy on the planet the next.

I was a Catholic when the Mass was said in Latin and the priest faced the altar and you beat back waves of terror while confessing your sins in a dark confessional to a disembodied voice — there were none of these namby-pamby group reconciliations. Look, I can still say the Act of Contrition by heart — *backwards*, if need be.

So I have paid my dues, and anyone who thinks I haven't better not say it around me. I am not a violent man, but that would really tick me off and I would mutter something unkind, which is a venial sin and might cause me to end up in purgatory.

I don't think you want *that* on your conscience.

In any event, now I'm a Catholic parent of three wonderful children. (By the way, since the vignettes in this book cover a period of several years, you'll notice different ages whenever I refer to my children and perhaps a seeming discrepancy or two concerning time periods. I'm not losing my mind. Honest.)

People outside the faith often ask me: Isn't being a Catholic parent the same as being any other kind of parent?

This is such a silly question that when I hear it, I want to throw myself on the ground and laugh long and hard. But I don't because I'd get grass stains on my shirt, plus it would be rude, and rudeness is a venial sin. Or if it isn't, it should be.

The fact is, being a Catholic parent — especially of the Baby Boomer variety — is a unique calling.

Sure, sure, we're fellow members of the Fully-Nurturing Generation, hip to bonding, Aprica strollers, dads who stay at home with the kids, which Power Ranger is which, and so on. But only Catholic parents find themselves chatting with the Ed Asner look-alike in the J. Crew fisherman's sweater who teaches their child at St. Columba School and wondering: Where have all the nuns gone?

Only Catholic parents know the special, ahem, joy of taking young children to Midnight Mass on Christmas Eve, only to have one of the little dears (so wired you'd think she was hooked to an IV drip of Folgers) shout during the homily: "Santa's bringing me Malibu Beach Barbie!"

Only Catholic parents know that if you ask a boy who just made his First Communion to drape an arm around his sister and smile for the camera, he will wear an expression that suggests his dog was just run over.

These and many other related subjects are discussed in these pages, with what I hope is some small degree of insight and sensitivity, and a large measure of affection.

By the way, I have not eaten fish sticks since 1965. And if you were to serve them to me today, I would probably lunge at you with a fork.

After which I would say a good Act of Contrition.

PART 1

♥

ROLE MODEL / MARTYR

You kids today, you don't know how lucky you are

One major failing of Catholic Baby Boomer parents is that they don't tell enough hardship stories.

Our parents used to tell great hardship stories, remember? They told stories about walking ten miles to school through waist-high snowdrifts. They told stories about getting up at 5:00 A.M. to feed the chickens and milk the pigs and slaughter the crops (you might want to check me on those chores, I'm not a farmer).

They told stories about working sixteen hours a day in a sawmill ("If you sliced off a finger, you just picked it up off the floor and put it in your pocket till quittin' time. Then *maybe* you'd see a doctor . . .").

Sure, sure, times have changed. But there are still any number of ways that modern parents can allude to gritty, hardscrabble childhoods of their own, and thereby induce the requisite feelings of guilt and unworthiness in their offspring.

A little speech like this ought to do it:

> You kids today, you don't know how lucky you are. Take those remote control TV clickers. You know, when I was your age, we didn't even *have* clickers.
>
> If you wanted to change the channel, you had to actually stand up and walk three or four feet to the TV.
>
> Lots of times the floors weren't carpeted, either,

so your feet could get pretty cold. And even if the floor *was* carpeted, generally it wasn't the deep-pile stuff, so it felt sort of rough and scratchy on your feet. Plus the floors were usually cluttered with books and games and stuff, so there was always a chance you'd trip and sprain an ankle if you weren't careful.

I'm telling you, things were rough back then. Pizza. You know, when I was a kid, you couldn't *even get pizza delivered to your home!* Hey, don't look at me like that! I'm serious!

If you wanted pizza in those days, you had to actually jump in your car and drive to the pizza parlor to get it. Sometimes the ride could take, oh, five or six minutes, depending on traffic.

Often, by the time we got home, the pizza wasn't even hot anymore, just sort of . . . lukewarm. But we ate it anyway. Heck, we didn't know any better.

What else? ATM's. You know when I was your age, we didn't even *have* ATM's. Honest. If you wanted to take money out of the bank, you had to actually walk inside and *talk* to someone!

I know, I know! Isn't that wild?

First you filled out something called a withdrawal slip, which I'm not even going to get into here, it's so complicated.

Then you stood in line behind these little velvet ropes until one of the people who worked for the bank — it seems to me they were called tellers — waited on you.

Can you imagine?! All that hassle? Just to get twenty bucks?!

I look back on it now and I think: "How did we *do* it?!"

Oh, I could go on and on. Telephone answering machines. This'll probably freak you kids out, but when I was your age, we didn't even *have* telephone answering machines.

You think I'm kidding, but I'm not.

This is how bad it was back then: If the person you were trying to reach wasn't home, you had to keep dialing until he *was* home.

You couldn't leave a message for him or anything. I remember one night I dialed my friend Timmy's house *four times* before someone answered the phone.

I still have calluses on my finger from that night. It turned out Timmy and his folks had gone out to dinner. Swell. Nice of them to let me know.

I don't know, life back then was so . . . draining. Even going to Mass was tough. You know, when I was your age, they didn't even say the Mass in *English*! Look at your face — I *knew* you wouldn't believe that! But it's true!

The Mass was in Latin, so you couldn't understand a word. Plus the priest had his back to you the whole time. So many times I'd be sitting there staring at his back and thinking: "Uh, ex-*cuse* me! I'm over he-re."

Everything is so different now. See that nice superhighway out there? What is that, I-83? You know, when I was your age, we didn't even *have* an I-83. If you wanted to drive downtown, you had to take Charles Street all the way. Now, you can probably make that trip in twenty, twenty-five minutes. But when I was growing up, it usually took a half an hour.

Think about that: cooped up all that time in your old man's Ford Fairlane, nothing to do but sink into the vinyl upholstery and listen to the AM radio.

You kids today, you don't know how lucky you are.

Please. Don't get me started.

A bedtime chronicle

In my sweetest dreams, I see a young child's bedtime unfolding like this:

At precisely 8:00 P.M., the child yawns, stretches, and announces: "Whew, I'm beat! Been going hard all day with the tricycle, the Power Rangers action figures, the coloring books, and the rest.

"Anyway, I'm off to bed. No, don't get up — I see you folks are watching *Murphy Brown.* I'll just slip into my jammies and brush my teeth and hit the sack by myself. Good-night now!"

In reality, of course, the process is considerably more, um, *involved*:

▲ 8:00 P.M. — Mom and Dad gently announce it's bedtime. Child reacts with startled, deer-in-the-headlights look, as if his usual bedtime is, oh, midnight and this is an astonishing turn of events.

▲ 8:01 — Child declares he's "not even tired!" and is "not going to bed, no way!" In a tearful diatribe, he accuses parents of being unspeakably mean and wonders aloud if he was adopted.

▲ 8:03 — Child wraps both arms around leg of coffee table, vows to remain locked in this position until parents rescind ridiculous bedtime edict.

▲ 8:04 — After child's arms are pried apart with crowbar, child flops to carpet in classic dead-weight, "limp-noodle" pose popularized by nonviolent protesters from Gandhi to the Berrigans.

In bizarre mood swing, child now declares he's "too tired" to walk upstairs by himself.

▲ **8:05** — Dad slings child over his shoulder and promptly pulls something in lower back, triggering lifetime degenerative disk problem.

▲ **8:07** — Child's pajamas are nowhere to be found. A lengthy search finds them balled up in corner of closet along with three partially-eaten Gummy Bears.

▲ **8:10** — Time to brush teeth. With painful and exacting deliberation, child squeezes toothpaste on toothbrush.

▲ **8:12** — Child is still squeezing toothpaste on toothbrush.

▲ **8:14** — Dad says: "Can we speed this up, buddy?" Child scowls, claims to be "hurrying as fast as I can."

▲ **8:16** — Actual brushing commences, with child using exhaustive one-tooth-at-a-time method. Dad dozes off from boredom, awakens to find child applying delicate, rococo swirls of toothpaste to bathroom mirror.

▲ **8:19** — Time for prayers. Impressively covering all the bases, child asks God to please help everyone from the poor, the sick, the starving, the homeless, orphans, etc., to the terminally dim-witted. In a bizarre addendum, child also asks God to watch over Mighty Morphin Power Rangers.

▲ **8:23** — Time for a bedtime story. Dad opts to read Berenstain Bears' classic *Too Much Junk Food*, skipping every other paragraph in order to move things along.

▲ **8:25** — Child wonders aloud about glaring gaps in plot continuity and character development in *Too Much Junk Food*. Demands to know what happened to climactic scene where health-food convert Papa Bear celebrates dramatic weight loss with carrot sticks.

▲ **8:30** — Child insists on *another* bedtime story. "Make one up, Daddy!" child implores. Dad stumbles through thoroughly unconvincing tale of this, uh, plucky little pig named, um, Ned.

Anyway, one day Ted ("Daddy, you said his name was *Ned!*") went off to seek his fame and fortune in the big city of, oh, Chicago . . .

▲ **8:35** — Child expresses appreciation for Dad's effort by calling the story of Ned, the plucky little pig, "the dumbest story I ever heard."

▲ **8:37** — Time for bed. Child is tucked in, kissed. Dad turns toward door. Sure enough, child asks for drink of water. Child takes tiny sip of water and asks: "Where does water come from?" Dad stammers through halting explanation of hydrologic cycle, including evaporation, precipitation, transpiration of plants, etc.

Child expresses his keen interest in the subject by ignoring Dad and playing with his toes.

▲ **8:39** — Child suddenly blurts: "Know who's the meanest kid in my class?" and launches into stinging indictment of young Jayson Montrose, who never lets anyone borrow his crayons and routinely trips his classmates.

▲ **8:43** — Lights out. Dad takes three steps out the door, only to hear child yell: "Dad! Come here — it's important!"

▲ **8:44** — Child says he takes back everything he said about Jayson Montrose. Child says that Montrose is an altar boy compared to Danny Clark, who

22

smacked Justin Fevrier at snack time. Speculation is that the thuggish Clark will occupy a dank cell in San Quentin by age eighteen.

▲ **8:46** — Lights out: the sequel. This time Dad makes it halfway downstairs before an unearthly wail emanates from child's room. Rushing back upstairs, Dad trips, bangs head against railing, setting in motion lifelong equilibrium problems and headaches.

▲ **8:48** — Child tearfully explains that a TV cartoon about monsters earlier this morning has left him frightened in the darkened room. Child asks Dad to lie down next to him for a while.

▲ **8:55** — Finally, sleep at last. Dad is out like a light. Child will be up until approximately 10:30 playing with his toes.

First Communion and photo opportunities

As these are *your* children — and let's face it, more handsome, photogenic kids never walked the planet — you will want to capture their every move on camera, whether still or video.

Some observations on parental picture-taking vis-à-vis little kids:

▲ When I said "capture their every move on camera," I did not mean that literally. No matter how adorable they look, we don't need to see twenty-six snapshots of little Janie making faces while perched on the potty (heh, heh) or Darren smearing strained peas on his face during the get-together following your oldest child's First Communion. In other words, don't be afraid to give the camera a rest. If you catch my drift.

▲ If you ask a child to smile for the camera, and the child does not *want* to smile, but you insist and make a big scene, the child will wear an expression in the snapshot that suggests you just beat him or her with a stick.

▲ Unposed photographs: Courtney being chased by an irate swan as she poses by a lake after her confirmation — look more natural, is what I'm getting at.

▲ Show a little imagination, for God's sake. Have the kids say something besides "cheese" when you take their picture. Even something goofy such as: "Please,

please, no more peas," which I heard a young father say at a Shriners picnic once.

▲ Don't be a pain in the neck at birthday parties, okay? If you're constantly interrupting the children with shouts of "Look over here, sweetie!" and "Blow out the candles again, buddy, I want another shot of that!" the children will start to hate you. Eventually, they will begin plotting to sneak into your bedroom at two in the morning with a can of Sunoco 190 and a book of matches. And no one could blame them.

▲ That pain-in-the-neck-with-a-camera business goes for baptisms, First Communions, and confirmations, too. Asking Father Jerry to pose with your family for one or two pictures after your child is baptized is okay — five or six pictures is pushing it, big time. The man is a priest, not a saint. I wouldn't be surprised if he hauled off and popped you.

▲ If you ask a boy who has just made his First Communion to drape an arm around his little sister and smile for the camera, he will look as though a large piece of bark is propped sideways in his mouth, forcing him into a painful grimace.

▲ The little girl, on the other hand, will wear an expression of pure joy. Little girls are great sports. Plus they just don't take a bad picture.

▲ A word or two about video cameras. I would not plunk your three-year-old on one end of a seesaw, then plop down on the other end, with the weight differential (let's say one hundred eighty pounds versus thirty) causing the child to catapult skyward in the manner of Wile E. Coyote in his Acme rocket launcher while you record the whole thing.

Even as a "hoot."

Save that stuff for those idiots on *America's Funniest Home Videos*.

▲ While most churches allow parents to videotape their child's First Communion, remember this: Cecil B. De Mille is dead.

In other words, you're not filming *The Ten Commandments* here. Don't make a spectacle out of yourself. Stay out of the way. Don't block the people behind you.

It goes without saying that any parent with a Sony camcorder who yells "Give us a big smile over here, sweetie!" as his daughter walks down the aisle should be beaten with sticks.

▲ Here's the lowdown on family portraits. The minute you arrive at the studio, everyone scrubbed squeaky-clean and dressed in his or her Sunday best, the following will happen:

1. At least one child will refuse to smile, no matter what silly faces the photographer makes or which handheld puppets he holds.

2. The ribbons that you spent twenty-five minutes tying in your little girl's hair will fall off.

3. A large cherry Juicy-Juice stain will suddenly make itself visible near the third button from the top of your son's shirt.

4. As soon as the photographer has the entire family arranged just so, one or more children will decide a visit to the bathroom is absolutely necessary.

5. In the finished portrait, at least one child will appear to be gazing at a point on the ceiling somewhere over the photographer's head. The other

child will appear so red-cheeked as to seem feverish, leading anyone who studies the picture to wonder what kind of parents would drag a child obviously in the throes of a major illness to a photo session.

Despite their brave smiles, both parents will wear a vague look of concern in the finished portrait.

Eventually, they will order only *one* 8x10 glossy, which will be strategically hung in a corner of the house where there is very little traffic. This is usually the laundry room, for some reason.

It's all over but the crying

There comes a sobering moment in every man's existence when he realizes he's already seen the best life has to offer, and that everything from this point on is a long, dark slide into the cold ground.

That moment has arrived for me.

I'm buying a minivan.

Plymouth Voyager, Toyota Previa, Dodge Caravan . . . what difference does it make? My life is over.

Four-speed overdrive transmission, 3.0-liter V6 engine, wood-grain side panels, extended luggage rack . . . so what?

What did the author William Styron call the gloom that came to envelop him? A veil of darkness descending slowly? Yes, I can see how that would fit.

There is an ineffable sadness associated with the sight of a man in a minivan.

When a man sits behind the wheel of a minivan, all pretense of being even *vaguely* hip vanishes.

Somehow — even before he sings out to the children: "Everybody have their seat belts on?" — he loses his identity.

He loses his soul.

He loses his swagger and his sense of cool.

He becomes a . . . *dad*, the doppelgänger of Homer Simpson and Cliff Huxtable and Dagwood Bumstead and a million other nameless, faceless wretches who exist solely (it would seem) to fire up the grill on weekends.

Teenage thugs snicker as he drives by, greatly amused by the minivan's bumper stickers proclaiming recent family visits to Aunt Bee's Gingerbread House or Walt's Famous World of Reptiles.

Single people stare in horror as he pulls up to the Dairy Queen and the minivan disgorges five brawling children (three of his own and two of the neighbors') for a tranquilizing round of chocolate shakes.

Women no longer glance over and smile as he pulls up to a traffic light. In fact, as far as *young* women are concerned, there might as well be a sign on the side of the minivan that says: "St. Joseph's Seminary."

A man driving a minivan becomes, for all intents and purposes, invisible.

Eagle Summit, GMC Safari, Mazda MPV . . . is this what it's all about?

Optional moon-roof, rear-wheel antilock brakes, swing-out and fold-down Dutch door . . . I guess it should matter. But it doesn't.

Sometimes, if I *really* want to feel low, I think back on the evolution of the cars I've owned.

There was high school and the Age of Aquarius and a succession of beat-up old Volkswagen Beetles with amateurish psychedelic paint jobs.

There was college, tuition struggles, and an economical Ford Pinto, the Death Machine, a young man praying that a soft tap from behind by a careless motorist wouldn't produce a towering fireball visible for many miles. Or that if it *did*, it would happen before his 9:00 A.M. Introduction to Chaucer class.

Then a few years later, it happened. I bought a brand-new Camaro. Metallic gold paint job. Black interior. Powerful V8 engine. Four on the floor. Hurst shifter. Zero to 60 in what — six seconds?

It was the greatest car a guy could own — until I drove it into a stone wall. How? Don't ask. It's too painful.

The repair job cost twenty-one hundred bucks. The garage should have sent a priest along with the bill, because the car was never the same. Six months later, it was sold to an earnest young man who announced he needed it to attend culinary school.

It didn't strike me as the kind of car a chef would necessarily favor, but the world was changing fast.

After that there was a sporty Nissan 200-SX, a wonderful car for a newly-married man except that it had all the leg room of the *Apollo 6*.

Then the newly-married man and his wife had a child, and then another child. It was time to buy a Subaru station wagon.

A *station wagon*, for God's sake.

The station wagon should have sent up a psychic flare that things were changing dramatically, that there was to be a great dimming to the joy of driving. Then a third child came along and suddenly it was an effort to shoehorn everyone into the station wagon.

Now it's a minivan.

Mitsubishi Expo LRV, Pontiac Trans Sport, Oldsmobile Silhouette . . . it's so hard to get out of bed in the morning.

Integrated child-seat option, heavy-duty upgraded upholstery, rear climate-control system . . . Gertrude Stein was right. There is no *there* there.

I go around to the various dealerships now. I

test-drive the minivans. I gaze listlessly at the brochures handed me by beefy salesmen in loud plaid sports jackets.

"Go ahead, take 'er out for a spin!" the salesman says cheerfully, tossing me the keys to yet another hulking seven-seater with all the sex appeal of a bakery truck.

"What's the point?" I think.

What was it that Nietzsche said: "A great-souled hero must transcend the slavish thinking of those around him"?

Sure. I wonder what he was driving.

The no-work zone

They say that by the year 2010, nearly half the country's workforce will work from home. Or maybe they don't say that — I'm a little shaky with statistics.

The point is, I don't see how anyone who works at home gets anything done, especially if you have a family and it's summertime.

I work at home a lot, and here's how a typical day goes:

▲ **8:00 A.M.** — I get my coffee, sit down at the word processor and . . . BAM! BAM! The coffee spills all over my lap. Something's banging against the door to my office. It's the dog. He wants to go out.

Any other dog would scratch at the door. But this dog is so stupid, he actually hurls himself against the door.

Then, reeling from the concussion, he staggers around like a sailor on a weekend liberty.

I'll tell you, seeing an animal do that to himself, that's a tough way to start the day.

▲ **8:22** — BAM! The office door swings open. It's the three-year-old, all jacked up from watching the Mighty Morphin Power Rangers. He aims a few roundhouse kicks at my desk and announces he wants a bowl of Cheerios.

Sometimes I look at this kid, and all I see is a cell door clanging shut behind him fifteen years from now.

I just hope they have Cheerios in the joint.

▲ **9:05** — The phone rings. It's the eight-year-old's

friend. The friend wants to know if there's swim-team practice.

I walk all the way upstairs to where my daughter is, find out practice is on, then pick up the phone.

"Yeah, there's practice," I tell the friend.

"Well, I'm not going," she says. "Swim team's stupid."

Lookee here! Apparently we found a future cellmate for the three-year-old.

▲ **9:44** — The doorbell rings. I run to get it and the dog bolts from the couch and attacks my leg. He thinks we're playing. He's still snarling and chewing my sneaker as I open the door.

It's two Jehovah's Witnesses. They're handing out literature about their church.

"Your church — is it quiet?" I ask them.

"Oh, yes," one young man says. "Very peaceful."

"No kids, no dogs?"

"Well, children *do* belong to our church," he says.

"Yeah, they belong to my church, too," I tell him. "So I might as well stick to Catholicism."

▲ **10:07** — My wife asks if I can watch the three-year-old for a few minutes while she runs to the supermarket.

Sure, why not? After all, I managed to write two whole paragraphs without any interruption. It's definitely time for a break.

▲ **10:09** — The three-year-old wants to play a board game: Candyland.

No, I say, Candyland only takes a few minutes. Let's play something like Monopoly that can take a couple of hours. That way I'll be *sure* to blow my deadline.

▲ **11:30** — The doorbell rings. I run to get it. This time the dog comes flying off the couch like some kind of vampire bat and latches onto my shirt. He's hanging there by his teeth when I open the door.

It's the kid next door. He's looking for the twelve-year-old.

"How come you're not working?" the kid asks me.

▲ **Noon** — Time for lunch and another well-deserved break. I've got exactly four paragraphs written. Hey, my editor's always telling me to write shorter.

▲ **1:20** — The doorbell rings. I run to get it. Sensing an imminent attack from the dog, I cover my head with my arms and plow blindly into the bookcase, cracking two shelves. This time, of course, the dog doesn't budge from the couch.

The guy from the lawn maintenance service is at the door. Apparently, he's already put down the weed-killer, since huge vapor clouds are rolling off the lawn and the smell of chemicals is choking.

"Don't worry," he says. "It won't hurt the dog."

"Yeah," I say. "That's what I'm afraid of."

On the other hand, I myself am thinking of slipping into a Mylex protective suit and oxygen mask.

▲ **2:05** — The phone rings. It's a local company that does home improvements.

"Well," I say, "can you fix bookcases? Because I just broke mine running away from my psycho dog."

▲ **3:12** — I hear the sound of a truck and bells jingling. A shiver of terror runs through me. Instantly, my body goes into full fight-or-flight response. It's the ice cream man!

Quickly I try to hide under the desk and . . . BAM! It's too late. The office door swings open. It's the three-year-old. He wants money so he and his thuggish little friend can score a couple of Jetstars.

To make his point, he karate-chops the printer.

I'm afraid of him, so I give him two bucks.

Although, to be honest, I'm even more afraid of the dog.

Maybe I'll knock off for the day.

Quality time? In a pig's eye!

The two of us were sitting on a bench next to the petting zoo watching our toddlers gawk at these four enormous pigs, when Jim snapped shut his Toshiba laptop and mentioned how happy he was to be spending "quality time" with his kid.

I hadn't heard that term in years, quality time.

Then again, I had never seen anyone bring a computer to a petting zoo, either.

Clearly, it takes a certain level of concentration to tap out a sales report with a bunch of two-hundred-pound pigs grunting loudly and jostling each other thuggishly for food.

Me, I need it quiet as 3:00 A.M. just to write "Don't forget dentist appointment" and hang it on the refrigerator with the little pineapple magnets.

As the two boys threw carrot sticks at the pigs — well, my kid was throwing *rocks*, prompting me to have a vision of a dank cell in San Quentin — I thought about this issue of how parents spend time with their children.

Sadly, many of today's moms and dads don't spend very much time with their kids at all.

According to a University of Maryland study quoted recently in *The Washington Post*, parents spend a grand total of two hours a day with their children, forty percent less than in 1965.

Fathers, in particular, have no reason to take a bow.

Your basic garden-variety dad talks *(talks!)* with

his kids for less than eight minutes a day. And he plays with the children or helps with their homework fewer than six minutes each day.

Clearly, for busy fathers like Jim, an executive for a pharmaceutical company, the problem isn't finding quality time to spend with the kids. It's finding *any* time to spend with the kids, leading to the bizarre sight of a man making his way through a rainbow coalition of livestock on a Saturday morning with a child in one arm and a briefcase crammed with work in the other.

(God knows what the pigs thought of all this. Although come to think of it, with the way so many parents are stressed out, they probably see it all the time.)

Quality time . . . how did this silly little term worm its way into our national consciousness in the first place?

To the whiny yuppies and starry-eyed New Agers who first coined it back in the 1980s, it meant doing something "meaningful" with your child, no matter how limited your time together.

Yet over the years, even the most dim-witted parent has come to realize that right behind love, time is the thing children need in abundance from their moms and dads.

Sure, it's all well and good to hustle the kids off to the circus or a ball game when you, as a parent, have an hour or two to spare. But it's more important that your kids know you'll "be there" (to resurrect another drippy eighties term) when they need you.

Not that you get to pick and choose the circumstances in many cases.

On a recent Saturday, for instance, I spent some quality time with my two-year-old, beginning at 8:00 A.M., when it was discovered that his diaper needed changing.

The discovery was made when a powerful odor suddenly filled the room, to the point where it was clear if the boy's diaper was not changed immediately, I would probably black out.

After the boy was dragged kicking and screaming upstairs — heh, heh, little fella doesn't like to be changed — he announced he wanted breakfast.

So we went back downstairs and I fixed him a nice bowl of Rice Krispies, bananas, and milk. He promptly signaled his gratitude by shot-putting the bowl across the kitchen.

This necessitated a prolonged cleanup session that found his father down on his hands and knees with a sponge, which apparently proved boring to the boy, who went off to watch Barney on TV.

Well. Here the day was young and already I had spent more than twenty-two quality minutes with him, far exceeding the national average (he said modestly).

If memory serves, it was at this point that the eleven-year-old and the eight-year-old appeared, in the midst of a vicious argument about who had bumped whom coming down the stairs.

It was a riveting conversation ("He hit me with his elbow!" "She tripped me!"), although I missed bits and pieces of it, since the Barney theme song emanating from the next room was now at a decibel level normally associated with the Concorde at liftoff.

Clearly, all three children and I were getting to know each other quite well — perhaps even a little *too* well — as by this time I was considering locking myself in the hall closet.

Anyway, we spent the rest of the morning doing yard work, with me handling the mowing and weeding and the kids mostly settling this burning issue: Could a stegosaurus beat a tyrannosaurus in a fight?

Total quality time spent with the children: a very respectable four hours, ten minutes, which did not merely exceed the national average, but so far surpassed it that I surely emerged as the strong front-runner for Parent of the Year.

We'll have to do it again real soon.

PART 2

♥

THE FAMILY THAT PRAYS TOGETHER

Your guide to
saner worshiping

Maybe the toughest decision a Catholic parent faces each weekend is: Which Mass should I take my kids to so that they obtain the maximum spiritual benefit while causing the least amount of embarrassment to me?

Now maybe some of you newer parents are thinking: "Wait a second. Aren't *all* Masses pretty much the same?"

No, I'm afraid not, Mr. or Mrs. Out-of-Touch. Each Mass has its own subtle flavor, and therefore attracts its own following:

▲ **4:00 P.M., Saturday** — Some years ago, the Church got tired of all the whining about how tough it was to get to Mass on Sundays when you were on vacation, out of town, attending a special event, etc.

So the Church said: "Fine, we'll let you go to Mass on Saturday, okay? And it'll count toward your Sunday obligation."

This shut up some people for about, oh, five minutes. Then pretty soon, all the Type A personalities were whining: "Look, having Saturday and Sunday Masses is fine and all, but we're very busy on the weekends. How 'bout some *Friday* Masses to count toward that Sunday obligation?"

Which is when the Church said: "Don't make us slap you. Because we *will* do it."

Anyway, the 4:00 P.M. Saturday Mass is the Children's Mass in many parishes. This means that three hundred little kids and their parents shoehorn into church; the noise level at times approaches that of a *Saturn V* rocket at liftoff. Which means this is not the Mass to attend if you're seeking quiet contemplation.

During Christmas and Easter, the homily may be given over to skits performed by the children: Mary, Joseph, and Baby Jesus that first night in Bethlehem, Christ's resurrection from the dead, etc. At least one child will forget his or her lines and, in a blind panic, turn and slam head-first into the altar.

▲ **5:30 P.M., Saturday** — Generally the most sparsely attended, this Mass is perfect for agoraphobics, sociopaths, members of the Federal Witness Protection Program, and anyone whose wardrobe consists solely of blue jeans.

If you're one of those Catholics who's *still* uncomfortable with exchanging handshakes and saying "Peace be with you" to strangers, you can generally sit ten pews away from the nearest person.

Since it's near the dinner hour and not far from bedtime, this Mass isn't usually popular with parents of young children. Bringing a hungry, tired three-year-old to church is the equivalent to strapping a dozen sticks of dynamite to your chest. Something bad is sure to happen.

▲ **7:30 A.M., Sunday** — Since the only people who enjoy getting up early on weekends are old people, this Mass is dominated by senior citizens. The odd teenager here was probably rousted out of bed at gunpoint.

On occasion, I have brought my three-year-old to this Mass; the sight of small children is so foreign that some of the geezers will actually stare at my kid and remark to one another: "What is that, a dwarf?"

Since there is no singing, you're in and out of this Mass in thirty minutes, which automatically puts the crowd in a good mood.

▲ **9:00 A.M., Sunday** — This is the most popular Mass for the parents of young children. Since the kids have been up for a while, they're lively and alert, yet not so hyper that they're running around like chihuahuas on methedrine.

When the collection is taken, half the moms and dads in church can be heard saying: "Okay, sweetie, give the nice man the money. Go on, put the money in the basket. No! No! *In* the basket . . ."

▲ **10:15 A.M., Sunday** — The marquee Mass attended by anyone who's important or thinks he is. The mayor and his family go to this Mass. Sprinkled throughout the crowd are men in two-thousand-dollar Armani suits, women in expensive Christian Dior knit dresses, and kids in pricey Polo sweaters.

This Mass is often a showcase for the choir, with the singers so pumped up you'd think they were auditioning for a gig in Vegas. Instead of being uplifted, however, the crowd is often surly, since all the singing tends to add an extra ten minutes to the Mass.

▲ **11:30 A.M., Sunday** — This Mass attracts procrastinators, teenagers who want to sleep late, and parents with young kids who are truly incorrigible, one step away from leg shackles.

For a good laugh, check out the poor parents behind the glass wall of the Crying Room, where the scene often resembles the chariot races in *Ben Hur*, only not that subdued.

▲ **12:45 P.M., Sunday** — This is the hard-core party crowd. Statistically, one in four suffers from a massive hangover. Some may actually arrive with party hats or bits of confetti still in their hair.

Even the ushers look like they've had a tough night. The man delivering the readings looks as if he might have slept on a pool table.

A wonderful Mass for the truly slothful, as it cleaves the day in half. A person can spend all morning in bed, go to Mass, and then spend the rest of the afternoon on the couch in front of the TV.

All together now —
uh, except for you

For the singing-challenged, there is that moment
— maybe it's a high note in "Be Merciful, O Lord" at
the 10:15 Mass — when it becomes clear that you are
doing something terribly wrong.

All around you is the sound of smooth, mellifluous
voices raised in perfect harmony.

And yet you keep picking up signs that your own
voice is somehow *different*.

Maybe it's a sharp glance from the woman in the
red dress to your right, who suddenly appears annoyed
at something.

Or maybe it's the teenager who keeps turning
around and looking at you the way he would at a fly
walking across his cheeseburger.

It might even be your wife, who leans over and pats
your hand and whispers: "Honey, maybe you shouldn't
sing quite so . . . vigorously."

Eventually it dawns on you: These people are not
exactly taken with your singing voice.

This is hardly surprising, since you have a voice
that sounds, for all intents and purposes, like a
refrigerator being dragged across linoleum.

Grating to adults, shrill enough to frighten small
children, it is a voice that could trigger the howling of
timber wolves from two hundred yards away.

And while it occurs to you that a person with such
a voice should have the decency to remain silent while
others commune with God, you are nevertheless moved

to express yourself in song on occasion by your desire to, well, *celebrate* the Mass with everyone else.

What, then, does the singing-challenged Catholic *do* in such a situation?

A friend of mine (a priest, as it happens) tried to console me once by saying that God does not care how well we sing.

"True enough," I said. "But everyone in *church* cares — at least everyone around me. You can see it in their eyes, in that pained look on their faces when I'm floundering through 'Let Justice Roll Like a River.'

"I don't know . . . when I start singing, everyone else's voice just sort of trails off. Then they look at each other with this puzzled expression, as if a manatee had somehow gotten loose in their midst and was bellowing loudly — that is, if manatees even bellow at all."

"I'm sure it's not *that* bad," my friend said.

So I invited him to sit with me at Mass one Sunday. Which is when he admitted that, yes, it *did* appear as if my singing was disturbing a considerable segment of the people around me.

Of course, being singing-challenged is hardly a new problem in my life.

At birthday parties when I was a boy, while the other children gathered eagerly around the cake and prepared to sing "Happy Birthday," one of the mothers would make a point of coming up to me and chirping as cheerfully as possible: "Maybe you'd like to, um, start passing out the paper plates!"

As a teenager, I'd be cruising in my beat-up Camaro, drumming on the steering wheel and singing along to, oh, "Help Me Rhonda." Suddenly the passenger in the front seat would lunge forward, snap off the radio, and blurt: "I'm sorry. It's just that . . . how 'bout those Yankees, huh?"

Naturally, the whole problem carried over into adulthood.

A few weeks ago at my son's preschool, during a special program in which a dozen dads and their sons danced in the front of the classroom as a scratchy tape of children's tunes blared from one corner, a teacher tapped me on the shoulder and said quietly: "We *do* the Hokey-Pokey here, we don't *sing* it."

These days, then, what little public singing I do is confined to church. But even that is not going well, as you can plainly see.

As I read the situation, there are three options available to today's singing-challenged Catholic at Mass.

The first is not to sing at all, which does not seem practical. As so much of the modern Mass is "song-driven," this approach reduces the worshiper to a semi-participatory role, similar to that of the caterer at a wedding reception who is *there*, yes, but only to keep a flame under the chafing dishes and straighten up the parsley sprigs.

The second option is to practice a form of non-audible singing, in which one moves one's lips but permits no actual sound to escape.

While this might cut down considerably on the number of annoyed looks drawn from the other parishioners, it seems soulless and dispassionate, even vaguely deceitful.

The third option is not to worry what others think,

to sing loud and free, to sing with joy and, gulp, *passion*.

I myself am leaning toward Door No. 3 right now, although this would have to be reconsidered if the woman in the red dress at the 10:15 Mass continues to shoot dirty looks my way.

She seems to be a very powerfully-built woman with a hair-trigger temper.

And God knows, we don't need a scene.

Mr. Big Spender

The man next to me at Mass last week tossed a one-hundred-dollar bill in the collection, which I probably passed out for, oh, no more than seven or eight seconds.

The man did not, it must be reported, make this wonderful contribution discreetly.

First he made a big show of opening his wallet, which looked heavy enough to use as a doorstop.

And when he dropped the hundred in the basket, it wasn't folded unobtrusively in half or in quarters so you might mistake it for a ten, say, or even a dollar.

No, he had that baby spread out nice and neat so everyone could see it. Plus the bill was so new and crisp that it made a loud, crinkling sound that could probably be heard in the next area code.

Boy, I'll tell you. The Church is always saying: "Love thy neighbor, love thy neighbor." Here I didn't even *know* this guy and already he was getting on my nerves.

I bet he was even getting on God's nerves, although luckily God was too polite to send down lightning bolts or engage in any other stunning pyrotechnics.

Anyway, if you don't count the fainting episode, I thought I handled the whole thing rather gracefully.

As soon as the man dropped in the hundred, I decided to act cool, as if I see people dropping hundred-dollar bills in the basket all the time.

So as the basket neared me, I stifled a nonchalant

yawn and reached smoothly for my weekly offertory envelope.

That's the beauty of a weekly envelope — nobody knows exactly how much you're throwing in the basket.

Heck, for all Mr. Big Spender knew, I was throwing in a hundred-dollar bill myself. Or even a two-hundred-dollar bill. I don't know . . . do they even *make* a two-hundred-dollar bill?

Then I discovered, after frantically tapping my pants pockets, that I had left the envelope at home.

To make matters worse, I had also left my money at home. And all I had in my coat pockets was a grand total of two quarters.

Believe me, if I'd had more money, I would have coughed it up. *All* of it. Because this was not going to look good, me tossing in fifty cents on the heels of the serious money plunked down by Mr. Sam Walton here, or whoever he was.

Still, there was no way out of the situation. As a thin sheen of perspiration formed on my forehead, I tossed the two quarters in the basket. Then I slinked down in my seat as far as possible, which left me at about eye level with the hymnbooks.

The usher was kind enough to pretend he didn't notice me throwing in fifty cents, but of course he did.

These ushers, they notice everything. It's just that they're taught in usher school to register no emotion during the collection, no matter how pitiful the sum tossed in by cheap, miserable vermin like me.

Still, in this case, I was surprised the usher didn't signal the priest to stop the Mass and then, in a loud voice, say to me: "Lemme me see if I have this straight.

This man to your right, this fine upstanding Catholic, a person who obviously *cares* about his religion, just put one hundred dollars in the collection basket.

"And you . . . I can't be-*leeve* this . . . you're going to follow this selfless, magnanimous gesture by tossing in a whopping fifty cents? Way to go, Money Bags!"

Don't think these ushers don't want to go ballistic and say something like that on occasion, either.

Luckily, they're professionals and that sort of behavior is frowned upon. Which is a good thing. Because you wouldn't want to throw five bucks in the collection basket one week and have some big usher with hairy knuckles and a gravelly voice say: "We've had our eyes on you, pal. How's about making it ten bucks this time?"

What I want to know is, after the collection is over, do the ushers get together and talk about what everyone put in the basket?

Because let's face it, that could be brutal, especially if you've gone through something like I went through. The conversation could go something like this:

"See the stiff in the blue trench coat?"

"Guy slinking down in his seat? Eye-level with the hymnbooks?"

"Yeah. Fellow next to him — wonderful man, had a saintly look about him, y'know? — tossed in a hundred. Then *that* character threw in fifty cents."

Look, I *know* God doesn't care how much you put in the collection basket.

Although to be on the safe side, there'll be a healthy upward readjustment in next week's envelope.

Peace be with me

Each Sunday morning, I attend Mass in a place that has all the calm of a street bazaar in Marrakesh.

This is a small, second-floor room sealed off by a glass partition from the rest of the church, a carpeted, soundproof gulag for parents with small children who are a bit too — let's see, how to put this? — um, a bit too *high-spirited* to sit quietly with the rest of the parishioners.

It's called the Crying Room, which is appropriate enough, since sometimes when I'm there with my two-year-old son, Jamie, I feel like sobbing into a Kleenex.

At times, when the place swells with twenty or so little kids jacked up on Coco Crispies and waffles, the noise level approaches that of an aircraft carrier flight deck.

Babies cry. Toddlers scream. Tiny toy trucks clang against metal radiators. Little fists clutching Barbies beat a tom-tom on the glass.

It is not unusual to see two boys wrestling over a blanket while next to them, a cute eighteen-month-old in pink OshKosh overalls suddenly bursts into a loud, impressive version of "Old MacDonald Had a Farm."

Over the din, muted cries of "Justin, honey, please don't do that!" or "Bethie, it's not nice to hit people!" can be heard from weary parents who all seem to wear that jittery, deer-in-the-headlights look.

When we parents turn to one another before

Communion and say: "Peace be with you," we're not fooling around. We really *mean* peace be with you.

Years ago — and I'm not talking the Eisenhower administration here, I mean even fifteen years ago — there was no such thing as a Crying Room.

If your child was not ready to sit quietly through Mass, you simply kept the little heathen home.

Or you brought the child and sat with everyone else and took your chances. Then as soon as he or she began acting up, you'd scoop up the child and begin the long, humiliating walk to the back of the church, during which every eye was fixed on you and the only question on everyone's mind was: Will the little brat end up in Leavenworth or Attica?

Then some deep thinker hit upon the concept of the Crying Room.

Apparently, the reasoning went like this: Instead of having loud babies and toddlers at Mass making everyone miserable, why not have a special place where these children could sit and just make their *parents* miserable? Yes, it was a splendid idea — unless you're the mom or dad up there who's downing fistfuls of Tylenol like they're cocktail peanuts.

On the door to the Crying Room of our church, a small sign reads: "Food not permitted. Baby bottles only." But as even the most touchy-feely, always-talk-in-calm-tones parent instantly recognizes, this is a free-fire zone; you survive using whatever method works for you.

Therefore, some parents (oh, not *me*, of course) attempt to sedate their children with all manner of snacks: Cheerios, Cheez-its, raisins, pretzels, etc.

Sure, the kid may be tipping the scales at one hundred twenty pounds by the time he's four, but at least he'll be a *quiet* fat kid. And maybe if he's occupied with a pretzel, he might stop howling long enough for the rest of us to hear the Gospel.

Look, I'm not saying it's right, but I know parents who would whip out a six-foot hero from Subway if it would keep the little dear occupied for fifty minutes.

If there is a universally unpopular figure in the Crying Room, it's the parent who lets his or her child get away with (figuratively, at any rate) murder.

This is the dad who thinks it's cute when his kid sprints back and forth, or throws an Evander Holyfield-like uppercut at a passing toddler. Or it's the mom who sits there flashing an eerie, Stepford Wives' smile while her kid rips a copy of *The Berenstain Bears and the Messy Room* from the hands of the little girl nearby.

Thankfully, though, most parents in the Crying Room understand it is our job to teach our children how to behave during Mass. It's a dirty, lonely job, but somebody's gotta do it.

Somebody has to teach them that this is God's House, and that God would prefer that we be quiet and respectful and refrain from smacking that little boy over there — yes, the little hoodlum in the Three Ninjas jacket — even though he *did* throw a karate chop at us first.

The fact is, we parents in the Crying Room recognize that ours is a temporary situation. We know that someday in the not-too-distant future, our little ones will be mature enough to sit through Mass without suddenly standing bolt upright and loudly demanding to know (in the middle of the Consecration, no less): *"Can a stegosaurus whip a tyrannosaurus?!"*

Off the top of my head, I'd say no. But I'm often wrong about these things.

PART 3

♥

TOO MUCH TOGETHERNESS

It's only a game

As every clear-thinking American knows, wiffleball remains our greatest backyard game, better than badminton or horseshoes or any other sissy sport where you don't even bleed.

Wiffleball is for anyone willing to shrug off a full-speed collision with the tool shed and six months of subsequent blackouts just to snare a grounder up the middle.

Look, if you're one of these crybabies who runs into a hammock while tracking a fly ball and gets yanked off his feet and then whines about spending three weeks in a neck brace, then maybe a wimpy game like croquet is more your speed.

But if you don't freak out every single time you're wheeled into an operating room — and let's face it, that's why they have anesthesia — then maybe you have what it takes to play this game.

Really, if you think about it, no other backyard game demands such a range of athleticism and dark, suicidal urges.

Shuffleboard? Please. I'm yawning. My eyes are starting to close. Frisbee? They should have buried that sport in the Age of Aquarius.

Lawn darts? That's it, I'm officially asleep.

The beauty of wiffleball is that it's a sport the whole family can enjoy — or it can lead to endless bickering and bruised feelings, as is more commonly the case.

Certainly, a sullen pall seemed to hang in the air during our first family wiffleball game this season.

The day dawned sunny and cool, perfect for that harrowing ride to the hospital should someone snap an ankle in one of the many holes the dog had dug in the backyard.

In the interest of saving time, I quickly chose up sides. The key here, of course, is to stack the teams heavily in your favor.

What you want to do is get a lot of young, athletic people on your team.

Ex-college ballplayers, Green Berets, varsity softball champs, combat nurses — these are the type of players you want in your lineup.

On the other team, you stick all the pencil-necked computer geeks, pasty-faced math teachers, guys who throw like girls, asthmatics, drunks, people with heart conditions, the wheelchair-bound, narcoleptics, women who are eight months pregnant, even babies.

Then you ask in a loud voice: "Okay, are these fair teams?"

Before anyone has a chance to respond, you run to home plate, grab a bat, and shout: "All right, we're up first!"

In this case, the teams ended up being me, my ten-year-old son, and my son's fourteen-year-old friend against my wife, our seven-year-old daughter, and our two-year-old son.

Naturally, my wife started whining that the teams "weren't fair," even when we pointed out the obvious advantages to having a toddler in your lineup.

I mean, the kid has a strike zone of what, six

inches? How do you pitch to someone like that? If the kid had any brains, he'd keep the bat on his shoulder and draw a walk every time.

But this kid . . . I don't know, you can't *talk* to him. Instead of crouching down like Rickey Henderson and making it impossible to pitch to him, he's swinging from his heels on every pitch.

I felt kind of sorry for him — but not sorry enough to ease up on him during his first at-bat. So I fed him three fastballs — WHAM! WHAM! WHAM! — and he struck out swinging. Didn't take it real well, either. Started pouting like, well, like a two-year-old, if you want to know the truth.

Things did not improve a great deal when my daughter came up to bat next.

"Remember, she's only seven!" my wife shouted.

"She's got a bat in her hands, doesn't she?!" I snarled.

I mean, what was I supposed to do? Let her take me deep just 'cause she's seven? How's that going to look when word gets around the neighborhood that little kids are rocking me for homers?

So — WHAM! WHAM! — I started her off with two fastballs that (with all due modesty) were nothing but a blur. Then I threw her a curve that broke somewhere out by the swing set.

She waved at it feebly for strike three and walked dejectedly away.

"Now she's all upset!" my wife yelled.

Look, my thinking here is: She's young, she'll get over it. Fifteen years from now, I don't see her sitting on a Scandinavian leather chair in some shrink's office, sobbing into a Kleenex that her life is a mess because Daddy once K'd her on an 0-2 fastball.

Anyway, along about the third inning, trailing 28-3, the other team walked off the field — just like they do every year.

Then my wife, who's the biggest crybaby of them all, accused me of running up the score and not playing fair and blah, blah, blah.

It's a wonderful game, wiffleball.

Although some people take it a bit too seriously for my taste.

The vegetable dilemma: Don't worry, be happy

The scene at the dinner table unfolds something like this: Mom places a nutritionally-balanced meal consisting of (for example) baked chicken, mashed potatoes, and string beans in front of the child. Grace is said. Already the air is thick with tension.

Noticing the string beans, the child recoils from her plate as if it contained the severed head of a groundhog.

Within seconds she announces: "I'm not eating those string beans."

Mom, her face set in a tight smile, says: "Sweetie, please, let's not go through this again . . ."

Dad, frowning and gripping the gravy boat a bit too tightly, adds: "Michelle, string beans are good for you. At least eat a *few*."

The child places exactly one sixteenth of a string bean on her fork.

She places the fork in her mouth. She makes a gagging sound. Then she lowers her head and spits the one sixteenth of a string bean onto her plate, in the process raking her hair through the mashed potatoes.

The parents, for some reason, take this as a sign of disapproval with the string beans.

Mom (voice rising): "Sweetie, I don't know what to do with you! You don't like peas, you don't like carrots, you don't like—"

Dad (banging his fist on the table): *"Michelle, you're gonna eat those string beans if we have to . . ."*

Congratulations. The meal is now officially ruined. The child lowers her head and starts sobbing.

Dad stalks off to the TV room, vowing to never again miss the first quarter of the Giants-Cowboys game "for this nonsense!"

Mom retreats into the kitchen, pale and shaken, making a mental note to call her mother for advice on the situation.

God in heaven. Thankfully, scenes such as this need not be repeated anymore — or at least not every day — as long as certain common-sense guidelines are followed:

▲ Do NOT tell a child that by eating vegetables, he or she will "grow up big and strong." If the choice is between growing up big and strong or tackling an evil-looking mound of lima beans topped with a two-inch-thick pat of butter, the child will usually opt to remain "small and weak" or even "wan and sickly."

▲ On a related note, do NOT tell the child vegetables will help him "grow up big and strong like your dad," if his dad is a tired, puffy man who, more and more, resembles an aging Rod Steiger.

In fact, this may well have the opposite effect on the child, leading him to conclude vegetables cause more health problems than prolonged exposure to strontium 90.

▲ Do NOT say something to the effect of: "Your little friend Maria eats *her* spinach." A hurried conference between the two friends near the teeter-totter the next day will ascertain that you lied shamelessly.

It will also confirm that Maria, in fact, has been

known to sprint from the dinner table and be found cowering in the hall closet whenever spinach is served.

▲ Do NOT place a forkful of (for example) cauliflower into your own mouth, smack your lips, rub your belly, and proclaim: "Mmmmmm, that's *delicious!*"

Meryl Streep, Robert DeNiro, and a few other card-carrying members of the Screen Actors Guild can pull off a scene such as this; the rest of us, sadly, sound totally unconvincing. Even if you deliver an Oscar-winning performance, you run the risk of the child saying: "Dude, if it's *that* good, *you* eat it."

▲ After quickly admonishing the child not to call you "Dude," it's time to play your parental trump card, which is, of course, bribery with chocolate pudding and whipped cream.

Note: If we can backtrack for a moment, I envision a whole lot of problems for you parents who constantly tell your kid, for example: "Eat your vegetables so you grow up big and strong like Michael Jordan."

Mark my words: One day, fifteen or twenty years from now, there will be a knock on your door and it will be . . . well, let's say it's your son, in this case.

In a voice cracking with emotion, he'll say: "You . . . you told me if I ate my vegetables I'd grow up big and strong like . . . who was it? Michael Jordan? Well, I ate my vegetables religiously and as anyone can plainly see, I'm a small roundish man with asthma who looks nothing at all like Michael Jordan but is instead often likened to a young Charles Durning.

"Mom, I'd say you owe me an explanation."

At this, your face will redden and you'll rush into the other room to collect your thoughts and turn off the game show on TV, the one with Chelsea Clinton as host. (Yes, *that* Chelsea Clinton. She's become a big star.)

Then you'll put on some coffee and the two of you will sit at the kitchen table, where you'll launch into a halting explanation of why you felt it was so important for a child to eat his vegetables.

You'll toss out dated statistics from the National Institutes of Health, cite studies reported in the *New England Journal of Medicine*, as well as anecdotal evidence that clearly showed the nutritional value of peas, carrots, and corn.

But none of this will impress your kid. He'll sit there puffing on a Marlboro Light, sullen and withdrawn, failing to brighten even when you say: "Besides, you do *not* look like a young Charles Durning. Whatever gave you that idea?"

But at that point, I'm afraid it'll be a little too late for pep talks.

Say amen; say good-night

Until recently, bedtime prayers in my house tended to go on a bit, as each of the three kids would ask God to bless (in no particular order): every member of the family, every relative, every friend, the sick, the homeless, people without cable, people with overdue library books, etc.

Maybe you see the basic problem here. It seemed fairly obvious these prayers needed to be a tad more . . . focused.

As it was, my wife and I found ourselves dozing off at the foot of the bed as each child's prayers became progressively more meandering ("God bless the trees, God bless the sky . . .") and arcane ("God bless Cody on *Step by Step*").

Now factor in the time Nancy and I spent reminding the kids to make the sign of the cross correctly, to not slouch as they kneel, to not whack each other with wiffleball bats, etc., and bedtime prayers were taking about as long as *Monday Night Football*.

Therefore, in an effort to move things along and get the kids into bed before one in the morning, the following, um, *suggestions* were made:

LET'S TIGHTEN UP ON THE NUMBER OF PEOPLE WE PRAY FOR.

This isn't meant to sound uncharitable, but we can't pray for everyone in the entire world. As I told the kids, prayers are very important, but we need to get our sleep, too.

I also pointed out that if Daddy stays up all night praying with them, he won't get enough sleep, either.

Then pretty soon Daddy's boss, Mr. Bigshot Editor, would wonder why Daddy was constantly nodding off in front of the word processor and banging his head onto the keyboard, instead of writing columns for the newspaper.

Then Daddy would lose his job and not be able to pay the bills. And then we would be saying prayers such as this each night:

"Dear God, please don't let the utility company shut off our electricity. And that tow truck was snooping around again — please don't let them impound our car. Amen."

LET'S CUT OUT ALL THESE PRAYERS FOR PETS.

One night it occurred to me (and I don't exactly have a mind like an IBM mainframe) that an inordinate amount of the children's prayers seemed to be for Pudgie the dog, Rusty the cat, Pete the parakeet, and the rest of the menagerie.

Look, I *know* kids love animals. But these pets seem to be doing pretty well all by themselves. I don't see where they need any extra help from God.

As I told the kids, look at Pudgie. All this dog does is eat and sleep. In fact, if the dog kept a diary, each day's entry would read like this:

"Dear Diary: Not much new. Ate well. Slept for twenty-two hours. Bye for now!"

One thing's for sure, this dog isn't going to die from stress.

My point is, the dog has a great life. The *last* thing he needs is anybody's prayers.

Are you kidding? If anything, *we* should be praying for a life like that.

WHILE WE'RE AT IT, NO MORE PRAYERS FOR INANIMATE OBJECTS, EITHER.

This one came about when the three-year-old started asking God to bless Thomas the Tank Engine, the famous cartoon tank. Well, I say *famous*, but only if you're of a certain age, in which case you're also mercifully unaware that Ringo Starr is the voice of Mr. Conductor.

Anyway, we were willing to let the Thomas prayer slide, but then the three-year-old started bending God's ear (so to speak) on behalf of Garfield, Bert and Ernie, and so on. It quickly got out of hand.

Left unchecked, we would have still been praying for Donald Duck and his nephews Huey, Dewey, and Louie as the sun came up.

DON'T BOTHER GOD WITH TRIVIAL MATTERS.

This means that (in our house, at least) it's considered bad form to ask God for an A in Friday's spelling quiz. Or a new Nintendo game.

Look, I don't presume to speak for God. But that's probably the kind of stuff that drives God nuts.

Here He is, wrestling with weighty matters such as drought, famine, pestilence, man's inhumanity to man, what went wrong with the British royal family, and the like.

And here's some kid from the suburbs of Baltimore bugging Him for "Donkey Kong Country."

If I were God, I would get a little ticked off about this.

And I would think (metaphorically speaking): "Kid,

God helps those who help themselves. Right now I'm up to my elbows in that tsunami that hit Japan and a volcano that's ready to blow in Iran. So if you want a new Nintendo game, you'll have to get it the old-fashioned way: by whining till your parents buy it for you."

No blood? It's a great party

As a parent, I always felt that for sustained levels of adrenaline-pumping anxiety, there was nothing quite like hosting a child's birthday party.

In many respects, the whole thing resembles a hostage situation. Suddenly all these wild-eyed, agitated little people burst in the door and your heart starts pounding. You're not exactly sure how long they'll stay or what they want.

All you know is, you have to keep them happy, otherwise there's no telling *what* they'll do.

Or so I used to think.

Then my daughter turned seven one day and invited eleven girls to our house to celebrate.

The girls had fun playing musical chairs and "Mother May I?" and took careful and determined (but not vicious) whacks at a piñata.

It struck me how polite and well-behaved they were, to the point where I finally put down the pepper spray we keep for these things.

Later the girls enjoyed cake and ice cream, and not once did anyone laugh psychotically and jab a plastic fork into someone's arm, or head-butt the person next to her for no apparent reason.

In other words, there wasn't that mess-hall-at-Leavenworth feel so often associated with these affairs.

Boys are different, of course.

First of all, I would not allow eleven boys in my house for *any* reason, never mind a birthday party.

A birthday party with eleven boys — I'd think about holding that baby in a reinforced bunker somewhere.

If there is a lull in a girl's birthday party, the girls will chat amiably among themselves.

Boys will pick up a fireplace poker and start jabbing the cocker spaniel. Or they'll start throwing roundhouse kicks at each other's heads. Just for something to do.

Boredom is the enemy of all children at a birthday party, only boredom whispers a little louder to boys than to girls. If that sounds sexist, well, I'm sorry, but that's the way it is.

Anyway, it was after the cake and ice cream at my daughter's party that I witnessed a truly amazing sight.

As Chrissie opened her presents, the other girls all stood politely around the table, oohing and aahing as each present was opened.

Boys will not do that — not unless you were to line them up a half-hour earlier and pass out Dixie cups with medication.

Okay, I'll *tell* you what boys will do in this situation.

When I was ten years old, I went to a birthday party for a budding young hoodlum named Joey Oblinger.

Toward the end of the party, Joey began opening his presents. And one of the presents was a bow and arrow set that some idiot parent had deemed appropriate for a boy who showed every sign of being the next Al Capone.

Oh, sure, the arrows came with those rubber

suction-cup things on the end. But as soon as we saw them, it was like a lightbulb came on over our heads, just like in the cartoons.

As Joey continued opening his presents, some of us slipped down into the basement with the bow and arrows.

Within seconds, the suction cups were pulled off to reveal nice, sharp plastic tips. Then we found another bow and started firing the arrows at each other. It was considered sporting to aim at a person's eyes back then; this was the early sixties, people didn't whine every time they were wheeled into the emergency room.

If you needed an eye operation, you needed an eye operation. It was that simple.

Anyway, we were shooting these arrows at each other and suddenly — you talk about knowing how a movie will turn out halfway through it — there was a piercing scream. One of the boys went down holding his eye.

I think they rushed the kid to the emergency room, but if they did, none of us was paying much attention. The way we saw it, there were still four healthy pairs of eyes to go around. So we just moved to a different part of the house and kept shooting at each other.

Finally, Mr. Oblinger told us to put the bows and arrows down, which we did, but then we found a dart board and four metal darts, which, to my way of thinking, was like leaving a loaded .45 on the coffee table.

But Mr. Oblinger took those away, too, saying he couldn't "trust" us anymore — although not before one of the darts went sailing into an autographed picture of Dwight D. Eisenhower.

Then we all sang "Happy Birthday" to Joey and ate cake and ice cream and went home. It was a great party.

Okay, I say it was a great party. But maybe not for the kid who caught an arrow in his eye. He could be walking around today with an eye-patch, I don't know. Or he could be working on his third cornea transplant.

I'm not saying *he* gets all misty-eyed at the memory of Joey Oblinger's party.

But the rest of us had a good time.

Eating out:
The clock is ticking

At some point, all parents delude themselves into thinking their children are ready to eat in a restaurant without causing a scene.

The thing to remember is this: No matter how well you prepare for the event, it may eventually degenerate into a hellish nightmare of hurled French fries, firefights with straws, and a shrill chorus of whining: "Where's the *fo-o-o-d*?"

The idea, therefore, is to get the children in and out of the restaurant before the other customers realize the potential danger they're in and become agitated.

Immediately upon being seated, remove all objects that can be thrown at other diners. Remove the salt and pepper shakers. Remove the sugar and Sweet'n Low. Remove the napkin holder, which, in terms of potential damage, is like a bowling ball and can lead to all sorts of nasty litigation.

Once the perimeter of the table is secured, leap to your feet and signal the nearest waiter.

If the waiter is not looking in your direction, go up to him anyway, yank him by the arm, and drag him back to your table.

Yes, he will be a little put off by this. But this is no time for niceties. You're dining with young children. Time is of the essence.

Now, then. In a calm voice, ask the waiter to please bring you some Saltine crackers.

If the waiter starts to say: "Gee, I'm not sure we

have any Sal—" grab him by the collar, pull him down to eye level, and say: "Mister, I don't think you understand what we're dealing with here. These kids are ticking time bombs.

"Not only are they hungry, but the little one missed her nap. Which means they're gonna be meaner than Texas rattlers if we don't get something in their stomachs, pronto."

When the waiter returns with the Saltines, open ten or so packets and put them in front of the children. Then inform the waiter that you're ready to order.

If the waiter says: "But . . . don't you want to see menus?" grab him by the collar and pull him down to eye level again.

Then explain that, when dining with very young children, there is no time for *menus*.

Explain that you're dealing with a twenty-minute window of opportunity here, during which the kids might *possibly* behave enough for everyone at the table to devour their meals.

Explain that after twenty minutes or so, the kids' eyes will begin to glow and their heads will begin spinning three hundred sixty degrees. At this point, they'll begin banging their little fists on the table and dueling with the silverware and doing God-knows-what-else.

Then tell the waiter: "Okay, here we go. The kids each get a grilled cheese sandwich, fries, and a glass of milk. Two club sandwiches for my wife and me, and two beers. As you can see by the way my hands are trembling, we need the beers immediately."

Okay, you've cleared a large hurdle. The waiter has

77

taken your order. Unfortunately, though, the food will not be here for about ten minutes or so.

Don't panic. Keep feeding the children Saltines. If they begin to get restless, play a game such as "I See the Color" or have them name the state capitals.

Sure, this might be a bit much for a five-year-old and a three-year-old, especially if they get off on the wrong foot by naming Dallas as the state capital of Texas.

But instead of rolling your eyes and saying: "No, no, AUSTIN!" just be patient and say: "Okay, how about Alabama?"

Look, who *cares* if they're giving the wrong answers? You're just trying to keep them occupied, is my point.

(Note: Under NO circumstances should you, as a parent, suggest the children sing to keep occupied. Because in all probability, they will pick "Bingo Was His Name-O," the most irritating song in history and one that will leave the restaurant as empty as if someone had just lobbed a grenade through a window.)

Okay, the food has arrived. A few tips: Eat quickly. I myself don't even bother to *chew* my food when I'm with the kids but simply force it down my throat.

This next part is very important: NEVER allow a young child to operate a bottle of ketchup, even when the child whines: "Mommy, I want to do it *myself!*"

Failure to observe this rule inevitably results in chaos. First, the child will tilt the ketchup over his fries. Naturally, nothing will come out. He will then give the bottle a whack. Now a huge glob of ketchup will cascade forth onto the fries, burying them as well as the grilled cheese sandwich.

The child will then screw up his face and announce: "I can't eat this! It's ruined!"

At some point in the next few minutes, the kids will stop eating and announce they're not hungry anymore.

Metaphorically, this is like a bell tolling. The meal is now officially over. Any second now, the kids will become restless and begin hurling fries at each other or making faces at the little old lady in the next booth.

Quick, there's no time to lose. Swallow whatever's left on your plate. Forget about coffee and dessert — that's what they have 7-Elevens for.

Pay the check.

Get out. Now.

Before it's too late.

Having a great time —
wish you were here

As I stare out the window, the sky is the color of dishwater and rain is falling in sheets and a single thought loops through my mind: "Good God, we're all doomed!"

Two families share this beach house at the Delaware shore. Between us we have five young kids. Quickly I say a silent prayer and turn to the Weather Channel. A smiling man in a navy blue blazer says it will rain all day.

I think: "Why is this man so happy? Doesn't he understand what a rainy day at the beach *means* when you're with kids?"

▲ 7:45 A.M. — Uh-oh, this is it. The kids come storming into the kitchen. Picture breakfast with the Green Bay Packers and you have an idea of what's going on here. Just what we need: five little kids jacked up on Honey Cheerios and Apple Cinnamon Rice Krispies cooped up inside all day.

"Better give 'em half-portions," I tell my sister-in-law, whose family is staying with us for the week. "Cut the sugar intake, maybe we have a chance to get through this."

But she says something about how they're growing children and breakfast is the most important meal and blah, blah, blah.

"Suit yourself," I think. "But don't be surprised when they get restless and start lunging at each other with curtain rods."

▲ **8:15** — Well, that didn't take long. Someone just knocked the clock off the wall with a football. It was a wooden clock with some sort of nautical theme and now it's shattered. I figure we're looking at one hundred fifty bucks to replace it, easy.

It's a rule of thumb at beach houses: The junkier the furniture and knickknacks, the more it costs when your kids break something.

Already I can picture some misty-eyed landlord telling me in a choking voice: "That . . . that clock has been in my family for more than two centuries."

▲ **9:02** — My wife, in that overly-excited, Florence Henderson-talks-about-Wessonality! voice that signals the onset of panic, tells the kids: "I have an idea! Let's play 'Chutes and Ladders'!"

The game lasts maybe ten minutes. Then the kids decide to resume doing cannonballs onto the couch from the first-floor landing.

▲ **10:55** — No, it . . . it *can't* be! From the living room comes the first strains of a song that is at once nauseating and eerily familiar:

There was a farmer had a dog
And Bingo was his name-o.
B-i-n-g-o,
B-i-n-g-o,
B-i-n-g-o,
And Bingo was his name-o!

Please . . . not that. That's the most annoying song of all time! What's next, "Do the Hokey-Pokey?"

"We're playing a dancing game!" my four-year-old announces brightly. This is why some animals eat their young.

▲ **12:40 P.M.** — We've played Scrabble, Candyland, checkers, and had lunch. It's clear the adults can't take much more of this. My wife suggests we take the kids to the indoor amusement center. She says it has kiddie rides, miniature golf, and a video arcade.

Fine with me. But first I'll have to get a ski mask and a gun and rob a 7-Eleven. Because that's the only way we can afford all this.

▲ **1:30** — We're at the indoor amusement center. Gee, this was a good idea. There's only, oh, nine thousand other bored kids here with their exhausted, hollow-eyed parents. The noise level approaches that of the infield at the Daytona 500.

My daughter asks if we can play ski ball. Sure, I say. Because I'm thinking: "With any luck, I'll get whacked in the head with one of the balls and black out and miss the rest of the afternoon."

▲ **2:20** — Let's see, we've played ski ball, golf, gone on the merry-go-round, the Caterpillar and Giant Duck rides, and had a few snacks. I'm handing out so much change, people think I robbed a toll booth.

▲ **4:00** — We're back at the house. It's raining even harder now. I need to lie down in a dark room. But my wife says: "Why don't you read a book to the little ones? It'll calm them down."

What am I, Mister Rogers? Nevertheless, I gather the kids and read the Berenstain Bears' classic *Go to Summer Camp*.

The kids signal their appreciation by saying: "THAT was a stupid book."

▲ **5:15** — From the living room comes a loud crash.

The kids were wrestling and bumped into the bookcase. A seagull figurine has smashed on the floor.

Cleaning up the pieces, I have a vision. In the vision, I'm peeling twenty-dollar bills into the hands of a sobbing landlord as he whispers: "I . . . I remember my great-grandfather giving me that seagull when I was a boy."

▲ **6:30** — Soon it'll be bedtime for the kids. Better yet, it's cocktail hour for the parents. I turn on the Weather Channel. The weatherman says tomorrow should be sunny and the high in the 80's.

I hate when they tease you like that.

PART 4

SISTER SAYS: THESE ARE THE HAPPIEST DAYS OF YOUR LIFE

What's wrong with this picture?

As the parent of a child in Catholic school, you may find yourself chatting one day with the Ed Asner look-alike who teaches your fifth grader.

And somewhere in the course of the conversation, as he puts down his fat-free yogurt and rolls up the sleeves of his Bugle Boy sweater while postulating that "teaching is all about communication, pure and simple," you may find yourself thinking: "Whatever happened to the *nuns*?"

The answer is: Nobody knows for sure. Like the Shriners and Fuller Brush salesmen and other seemingly indispensable groups of another time, the nuns just seemed to fade away.

All of a sudden, around the mid-1970s, it seemed as if most Catholic schoolchildren were being taught by wholesome-looking women in Annie Hallish blazers and skirts and earnest men with thinning hair who wore white shirts, blue patterned ties, and gray slacks.

Sure, sure, these lay teachers were incredibly dedicated. But they failed to bring to the educational setting the essential ingredient that only a nun could provide, which was, of course, fear.

Let's face it, it was fear that made you study the Magna Carta, fear of being called on to explain it in class, giving some ridiculous answer and having Sister slam that yardstick on your desk with a loud WHAP! as she barked: "That is *not* correct!"

And it was fear that helped you memorize the

atomic symbol for boron, fear that if you didn't know it, Sister might lose it right there and whack you upside the head with that huge prayer book of hers, the one that was about the size and weight of an anvil.

Without fear, there is no learning, or at least not the panicky, please-God-let-my-brain-be-an-IBM-mainframe kind of learning that lasts a lifetime.

Clearly, Sister was way ahead of her time. Today, people who preach this learn-or-else gospel to workers at AT&T or the Ford Motor Company earn ten thousand dollars per speech and are called "motivational speakers."

Catholic school was a series of Kodak Moments for me; my image of Sister now is as clear as it was more than twenty-five years ago.

I see her in that forbidding black habit with the rosary beads swinging like thick lengths of bridge cable, a permanent head cold that left her cranky for days on end, fifteen wads of Kleenex stuffed up her sleeve and those steel-toed workboots.

Okay, maybe they weren't steel-toed workboots, I don't know. You could never tell *what* kind of shoes Sister wore. To tell you the truth, I was afraid to let my eyes linger on Sister's shoes, for fear that she'd spot me and fix me with an icy stare and say: "My, we have a lot of free time on our hands! Maybe we'd like to wash down the blackboards again . . ."

Yet as intimidating as she looked to a jittery fifth-grader, there were times when Sister could be the most pleasant person in the world.

When the conversation turned to the Monsignor, the Pope, Mother Superior, the saints, the Vatican, or the classroom's new movie projector, Sister would nod and smile and even laugh on occasion.

But let someone in the class act up or say something stupid, something like "Mickey Mantle is the greatest human being of all time," and the expression on Sister's face would change instantly.

It reminded me of a squall slamming into a New England fishing village; one minute there's sunshine and blue skies, the next minute darkness and rain and howling wind.

Seconds later the yardstick would come crashing down on someone's desk like a thirty-two-ounce Louisville Slugger — WHAP! — and we knew the good times were over. It was time to get serious again. Time to learn. And learn we did.

I liked Sister a lot, I really did. But I was afraid of Sister, too. Very, very afraid.

These kids who attend Catholic school today, they're not afraid.

I watch them in the classroom, their features relaxed, their eyes calm, their smiles serene. Heck, nobody even cringes anymore when they give a wrong answer to the teacher. I see all this and it makes me think of that old game: "What's Wrong With This Picture?"

I guess it's hard to be afraid of a kindly-looking man in a twill shirt and khaki Dockers helping you solve a problem on the computer. And the smiling woman handing back test papers in the platter-collar blouse and belted skirt from J. C. Penney, the one who looks like your favorite aunt; she's not going to intimidate a child, either.

Sometimes I miss Sister, I really do.

Although I sleep a lot better now than I did then.

Keep telling yourself:
It's only a dream

Journal of a back-to-school shopping trip:

▲ **11:00** A.M. — Arrive at mall. Gee, I'm glad we picked Saturday to do this. The nearest parking spot is somewhere in Vermont. A woman in a white Taurus cuts me off and noses her car into a handicapped spot. Then she leaps out and sprints to the entrance faster than Jackie Joyner-Kersee.

Way to go, lady. Why should the disabled hog all the good parking spots, right?

▲ **11:10** — We made it to the front entrance. Good God, the place looks like Woodstock! Anxious mothers drag sullen children from store to store. Jittery husbands with that deer-in-the-headlights look sit wearily on benches. Babies wail. Disaffected teenagers with shaved heads and nose rings hang outside the video arcade making snappy conversation with passersby: "Dude, you got a cigarette?"

My wife seems fine, but I'm white-knuckling the baby-stroller already. We stop at a water fountain and I knock back two Tylenol, steeling myself for the ordeal to come.

▲ **11:22** — Inside the Gap, snatches of conversation drift over the din:

Parent: "Now *this* is a nice jacket . . ."

Kid: "I hate that jacket."

Parent: ". . . that would go with this shirt."

Kid: "I hate that shirt."

▲ **11:45** — The twelve-year-old says he needs a

backpack. He picks out one big enough for scaling the north face of the Matterhorn. What do the kids *put* in those things: coffee pots, frying pans, Sterno? As the price tag flutters into view, I feel my heart stop.

Then I have a vision of my son ten years from now, sitting on a folding chair in a drafty church basement, sobbing to his support group: "The first time I sniffed glue? Probably when my dad wouldn't buy me that backpack. I felt so *rejected* . . ."

▲ **12:05 P.M.** — The six-year-old is picking up the essentials: Lion King pens, Lion King notebooks, Lion King folders, Lion King whatever else. I guess it wasn't enough that the Lion King people made a gazillion dollars off the movie. Maybe I could get a second job on a loading dock so we could hand over even *more* money to them.

▲ **12:16** — The twelve-year-old is shopping for loose-leaf binders when we come across one with a picture of Slash from Guns 'N' Roses.

Say, there's a great role model! Let's see, he's been in and out of rehab, charged with assault, arrested for public drunkenness . . . who're we putting on these binders next, Ted Bundy?

▲ **12:23** — Quickie update on this year's hot school look for girls: flannel shirts and overalls with one shoulder strap unfastened. A kind of Drew-Barrymore-meets-the-Berenstain-Bears look.

Very hip. I guess. I wouldn't know hip if it whacked me over the head with a two-by-four.

▲ **12:40** — Time for lunch. We head up to the food court, which has all the calm of a fish market in Hong Kong. We mosey over to the noveau pizza place. They have pizza with broccoli, pizza with spinach, pizza with pineapple, pizza with shrimp, you name it.

I ask the guy for four slices with pepperoni, he looks at me like I asked for Quaker State 10W-40 on the pizza.

▲ 1:13 — The twelve-year-old wants a pair of Reebok basketball shoes like Shaquille O'Neal wears. I look at the price tag and inform the salesman that there must be some mistake, that apparently this is the price tag from a twenty-seven-inch color TV.

No, he says, that's how much they cost. This time I don't care how much the kid whines to his support group ten years from now. The answer is no.

▲ 1:35 — We're in the Gap for Kids when I say to the six-year-old: "How 'bout a nice white blouse and corduroy jumper?"

She looks at me like I suggested a Big Bird T-shirt with Bert and Ernie coveralls. Then she starts eyeballing Madonna-like lace leggings for that classy visiting-my-boyfriend-in-jail look.

That should go over real well in second grade. I might as well head home right now and wait for the principal to call.

▲ 1:50 — Uh-oh, big mistake. I've wandered into your standard, neo-hip record store where something from Green Day is screeching over the sound system. A seventeen-year-old with dual nose rings is slam-dancing to the beat behind the cash register. The customers wandering up and down the aisles look like extras from *Night of the Living Dead*.

It's the closest I've ever been to a near-death

experience — only without the shimmering light and warm feeling of calm said to accompany it.

▲ **2:00** — It's definitely time to leave. The kids seem okay, but my wife has dark circles under her eyes. Me, I think I'm developing facial tics.

Once inside the car, I lock all the doors and stomp on the accelerator as we go fishtailing out the main exit.

Saigon is falling and the last chopper is lifting off.

It's a small world after all

For the parents of young Catholic schoolchildren, autumn is a stressful time, beginning with that crippling odyssey known as Back-to-School Night.

This is when parents visit their child's classroom at St. Ignatius the Tired and sit hunched at the child's tiny, cramped desk and lose all circulation in both legs as the teacher explains what the class hopes to accomplish throughout the new year.

The talk is invariably upbeat. With eyes glowing like twin coals and June Cleaver smile firmly in place, the teacher sprinkles her address with phrases such as "a new beginning" and "the uniqueness of each student" and "the individual worth of a person loved by God."

She may also take the opportunity to extol the virtues of a Catholic education, how it provides value-centered teaching and discipline and generally ensures that students will not grow up to don ski masks and wave guns in the face of startled convenience-store clerks at 3:00 A.M.

At this point, if you're like many parents, you may find your attention wandering from the crucifix on the wall to the statue of Mary and the Baby Jesus to the "Reading Is Good!" poster and eventually to thoughts of: "I . . . I think I'm going to pass out . . ."

This is because it is always no less than 110 degrees in the classroom. Plus every few minutes, you feel the urge to cry out as your knee slams into a bolt sticking out from the bottom of the tiny desk, until finally a small pool of blood seeps through your tan Dockers.

In a day or two, the wound will redden and swell and there will be talk of tetanus shots and *staphylococcus aureus.*

Yet the threat of massive infection is but one of the many annoyances you face right now.

There's always one gabby mom who is somehow impervious to the fact that the room has the same breezy feel as a mango grove in Panama, and who feels compelled to regale the teacher with her own lofty theories on education. ("Hand puppets help the children stay engaged, don't you think? When we lived in California, all the schools used them.")

There's always one adrenalized, Type A dad who gets beeped and rushes from the room like he's the Secretary of Defense and Saddam Hussein's troops have been sighted stockpiling processed plutonium.

At about this time, as the teacher holds up a copy of the *This Is Our Faith* religion text, muscle spasms begin shooting up and down your back as you sit hunched over at a desk apparently designed for the Keebler Elves.

Even more depressing, you'll be struck by the realization that you've somehow become responsible for all the various fund-raising activities your child is expected to participate in.

The money is needed for (check one):

❏ New playground equipment.
❏ New computers.
❏ New musical instruments.

❏ A field trip to the Smithsonian museums in Washington, D.C.

   ❏ [Other]_____.

The need is always urgent. It is made clear to you that without the new playground equipment, new computers, new musical instruments, etc., the children will languish and become dispirited, losing even more ground in the education race to their Japanese counterparts before eventually turning to drugs and a dead-end life of straightening up the salad bar at Wendy's.

So *you* must help your child raise money.

You must bring the candy bars into your office and try to nab a few suckers with a crude cardboard sign that says: "All proceeds go to St. Ignatius the Tired for new computers!"

You're the one who will have to "be there" for your kid at school-sponsored car washes, bake sales, fashion shows, pizza-selling campaigns, and magazine-subscription drives.

Your life will never be the same again.

All this occurs to you as you sit there at your child's tiny desk in this stifling room and, sure, it's unnerving.

But even more alarming is the fact that you have now lost all feeling from the waist down.

Although if you look on the bright side, this may keep you out of a few bake sales.

Words to live by

If I could offer one piece of advice to you moms and dads planning to speak at your kid's Career Day class, it would be this: Never follow a policeman.

Believe me on this one. Following a cop breaks the time-honored Theorum of Career Day Presentations, which states: (a) Kids are fascinated by cops. (b) They find every other job hopelessly dull by comparison.

So unless you're an astronaut or a Power Ranger following that cop, be prepared to see the whole class yawning and staring out the window as you die a horrible, sweat-soaked death at the blackboard.

This is basically what happened to me some time ago when I spoke to the third-grade class on Career Day at St. Patrick's.

Initially I was radiating confidence — at least until I walked into the classroom and noticed the other speaker, when I remember thinking: "My life is over."

Because in this case, not only was the other speaker a policeman, he was also a SWAT team member.

Which means he was dressed in one of those black Ninja-type outfits, with the hood and the boots, the whole nine yards.

Just in case there was any doubt about who he was, SWAT was spelled out in foot-high yellow letters on the back of his outfit.

To make matters worse, the guy had brought along all sorts of neat visual aids: sniper rifles, pistols, bulletproof vests, Mace, handcuffs.

What was I going to show the class — a ballpoint pen?

At this point, my only hope was that the teacher would let me speak first.

That way I could put the class to sleep and get out before the cop started speaking, at which time it would become even more apparent just how boring I had been.

Naturally, this hope was quickly extinguished when the teacher said: "Officer Charleston has a very important assignment to get to. You don't mind if he speaks first, do you?"

"Oh, absolutely not," I said.

For a moment, I considered taking a whack at the teacher right there.

But with that goody-goody Officer Charleston in the room, my chances of getting away with it weren't too good.

Anyway, Officer Charleston got up there and naturally he dazzled the class from the get-go.

First he told them about all the training that went into his job: his hours on the rifle range and obstacle course, how he learned to rappel down the sides of buildings, his work with the bomb squad, etc.

Then he told all these great stories about hostage situations he'd helped defuse and deranged gunmen he and his squad had captured.

Then he showed the kids his weapons and the bulletproof vest and everything else. He even handcuffed a couple of kids together.

Yes, he was a big hit, Officer Charleston was.

At the end of his talk, the kids were clapping and cheering and asking him for autographs.

Their little eyes were glowing and their little cheeks were flushed, and as I watched the little brats, one thought kept going through my head: "There is no hope — I'm doomed."

Now it was my turn to speak.

"Well," the teacher said, "I'm sure our next speaker will be every bit as entertaining as our last speaker."

"Don't count on it, pal," I thought.

Anyway, I started off by giving them ten minutes of drivel about what a columnist does, how the columnist crafts his column on the word processor, where he gets his ideas, blah, blah, blah.

It was so boring that even I was having problems staying awake.

At one point, I actually caught myself nodding off in mid-sentence, which none of the kids seemed to mind, since many of them were asleep, too.

Then I opened the floor to questions.

The first was from a charming little boy in the front row, who asked: "Were you ever a policeman?"

"Uh . . . no," I said.

Obviously we were off to a fine start.

The second question came from a little girl with freckles.

"Did you ever want to *be* a policeman?"

Clearly, the kids had been riveted by my descriptions of a life in journalism.

For a moment, I considered asking the teacher if we could all jump aboard a bus and try to catch up with Officer Charleston, in lieu of my spending the rest of the class answering police-related questions.

Which is pretty much what I ended up doing, to the

point where the kids were practically calling me Officer Kevin.

I told the teacher I'd be back for Career Day next year.

But this might have to be, um, re-thought.

PART 5

♥

COPING WITHOUT THERAPY: THE EARLY YEARS

Here's a shot of Timmy with our dog Zeth . . . Timmy's the one on the right, of course . . .

One problem with being around young parents is that they will often sit you down and *demand* (there is no other word for it) that you look at baby pictures.

There is a certain procedure one should follow here so as to avoid bruised feelings on the part of all concerned.

Upon seeing the first snapshot of the baby, immediately say something to the effect of: "Awwww, how cute . . ."

This will instantly put the parents at ease, and they will be eternally grateful that you didn't point out that the baby strongly resembles a honeydew melon with eyes, as they had originally feared.

The fact is that a good portion of today's babies are flat-out ugly, there is no getting around that. Yet sitting there on the sofa between the proud parents, a photo album on your lap and two glasses of Chablis warming your insides, you would not dare mention (even in passing) that the kid seems perfect for the lead role in *Mr. Magoo: The Early Years*.

Just once I would like to see someone glance at a snapshot of a baby, stiffen noticeably, and blurt out: "Marge, honey, I *hope* this is a picture of your cocker spaniel . . ."

That reminds me of an incident that took place not

long ago when I found myself at a wedding reception with two hundred drunks doing the Hokey-Pokey.

This is neither here nor there, but my philosophy on the Hokey-Pokey is simple: There is not enough booze on the planet to get me to do that stupid dance.

If you get a kick out of that nonsense, fine, knock yourself out. Just don't drag me into your insanity.

In any event, I was sitting at my table minding my own business when the couple next to me struck up a conversation. Maybe they thought I was bored or something, although I assured them that I *always* bring a twelve-inch color Sony to social functions.

Whatever the reason, this couple was really chatty, to the point where I could barely follow what was happening on *Wheel of Fortune*. Even when I turned up the volume, they didn't get the hint. They just kept talking and talking, the gist of the conversation being that they had just had a baby four months earlier.

Then came the moment I was dreading: The woman reached into her pocketbook and pulled out a stack of baby pictures.

Let me say this: I have seen a lot of babies in my time. I have seen fat babies and thin babies. I have seen cute babies and babies so ugly you figured they were raised by great apes.

But this was absolutely the *ugliest* baby I had ever seen. Oh, Lord, he was a homely little cuss! All I kept thinking was: "It's a good thing this couple left the baby home." Because if they had brought this kid to the wedding, you would have seen people stampeding for the exits all night long.

Believe me, if I had to sit next to this kid, I'd even

think about doing the Hokey-Pokey — booze or no booze. Anything to get away from this baby. I know that's a tough thing to say about a baby and it gives me no great pleasure to say it.

But there's no way to sugarcoat the issue. The baby was seriously ugly. And here I was, staring at a snapshot of the kid, the parents searching my face for some sort of reaction.

The dilemma was obvious: Do I go with my gut instinct (honed considerably by three Budweisers) and blurt out that the kid looks like a young Ernest Borgnine, which would send the young mother fleeing tearfully in the direction of the restrooms and possibly precipitate a brawl with the father?

Or do I lie shamelessly (as usual) and say the child is adorable, thereby keeping peace at the table and, with any luck, watching the last few minutes of *Wheel of Fortune* uninterrupted?

In an instant my mind was made up.

Gazing at the snapshot, I mustered what I hoped was a benevolent smile and said: "Awwww, how cute . . ."

This is how I recommend handling all similar situations involving baby pictures.

Especially if you're trying to watch TV. God knows there are only so many good sitcoms these days.

It's a dirty job,
but somebody has to do it

As a boy, I was taught to endure and persevere and never bother God with little things, and so I have not asked for His help in this matter, although every once in a while I raise my eyes to the heavens and think: "Maybe if You have a minute . . ."

This is what potty-training a three-year-old does to a person. I was once a fairly patient man, affable and slow to anger. Now, if you even *look* at me funny, I might bite your nose off.

People say: "Your three-year-old is potty training? That must be so exciting!"

Well, I . . . I *guess* it is, except for one small problem, which is that the three-year-old is more like three and a half and does not seem terribly excited about the whole business.

In fact, he seems content to remain in diapers until he's, oh, seventeen. The other day I said to him, in that overly-excited, Barneyish voice you tend to adopt for this sort of thing: "You know, going on the potty is fun!"

Sure, it was a ridiculous statement. I realize that now. But at the time, I was changing his diaper because he had just, uh, done something, if you catch my drift. And I was trying hard not to pass out, as there was now a rather strong odor in the room, so I kept telling myself: "Keep talking, keep talking, try not to breathe."

"Don't you want to go to the bathroom like a big

guy?" I continued, this time with a bit more urgency, because now the room was starting to spin.

"No," he said.

Which I'm sure was an honest answer, although not the answer I was hoping to hear.

If you're interested in these things — and I don't see why you *would* be — my wife and I potty-trained our two older kids the old-fashioned way: by bribing them.

We gave them M&M's every time they sat on the potty. They didn't even have to *do* anything, just sit there. When they *did* do something, we gave them even more M&M's.

Sure, they'd be vibrating like a gong from all the sugar. But at least they went to the bathroom by themselves.

But this three-year-old, he doesn't want to hear about M&M's or anything else. You could wave a twenty-dollar bill in his face and say: "This could be yours, sport, if you sit on that potty," and he'd simply ignore you.

A few months ago, we read him a book about toilet training called *I'm a Big Kid Now!*

In the book these two little cartoon brats, Jimmy and Amy, explore the wonderful world of toilet training and find it to be just oodles of fun.

They have fun sitting on the potty, fun relieving themselves, fun using toilet paper, and fun helping Mommy and Daddy clean up afterward.

I could tell that this book impressed our three-year-old, since, the moment I finished reading it to him, he said: "That's dumb!" and walked away.

Then we bought him this really cool potty especially designed to appeal to reluctant toilet-trainers. It has its own toilet-paper holder and a little rack to hold books.

It even has a little bell to summon Mommy or Daddy once the little dear is through, um, having fun.

Well. Not only wouldn't the boy sit on the potty, he wouldn't even *look* at the potty. When I pulled it out of the box for the first time, he ran screaming from the room, like I was showing him the severed head of a water buffalo.

Then we went out and bought him some cool underwear. We bought Batman and Power Ranger and Sonic the Hedgehog underwear to show him what "big boys who go on the potty" wear. I'm telling you, this underwear was so snappy-looking, I felt like slipping on a pair myself.

But this only moved the boy to a rambling soliloquy of why he wanted to continue wearing diapers, the gist of which was: Underwear is very overrated.

Look, we don't want to pressure the boy. Because that's the other thing the experts tell you: The more you pressure him, the more he'll resist. Plus all that pressure will surely lead to deep, psychological scarring, which will culminate in him lying on an analyst's couch thirty years from now, sobbing into a Kleenex: "I . . . I wasn't ready and they *made* me sit on the potty!"

So that's basically where we stand, progress-wise, in the boy's potty-training, although every once in a while we see him jumping from the potty and flapping his arms as if attempting to fly.

My wife says that's a good sign.

Me, I worry that he hasn't quite grasped the concept of what we're trying to do here.

Three years old: It doesn't get any better than this

If I had it to do all over again, I'd come back as a three-year-old, because three-year-olds have the greatest life in the whole world.

First of all, when you're three, you get to sleep as late as you want. If you roll out of the sack at ten in the morning, that's fine.

Nobody shoots you a dirty look. Nobody tells you to cut your hair and get a job. Nobody makes snide comments about how you should be doing something with your life.

Nobody hassles you about taking a nap when you're three, either. In fact, they actually encourage napping, which will be the last time in your life that this occurs.

Let's face it, if you're an adult and you fall asleep on the couch on a Saturday afternoon, that peace and quiet won't last long. Pretty soon someone will be yelling at you to get off your duff and rake the lawn or drag the snow tires up from the basement.

Or else the phone will ring and it'll be some guy trying to get you to take another credit card.

But when you're three, you can grab some shut-eye whenever you want. Your folks will actually smile if you trudge into the kitchen and announce: "Boy, the Big Wheels knocked me out! Think I'll take a little nap."

Nine times out of ten, they'll even carry you upstairs and tuck you in. Then they'll make sure the shades are drawn and the house is quiet. And if anyone makes any noise, your folks will hiss "Shhhh," as if it were Mother Teresa sleeping in the next room.

The only time an adult gets that kind of treatment is when the doctors tell him he's got three weeks to live.

Another neat thing about being three is, you get to wear the coolest clothes. I'm talking specifically here of those neat overalls, OshKosh and what have you, which you can wear without anyone calling you a hayseed or a rube and wondering what turnip truck you dropped off.

It's the same thing with underwear when you're three: Anything goes. If you're an adult and people see you changing out of, say, Mickey Mouse undies at the racquetball club, they're going to look at you funny.

But when you're three, you can wear Superman or Lady Lovely Locks underwear and it's considered a fashion statement. In fact, people will actually *compliment you on your underwear*! They'll see you changing and say: "Hey, what do you have there, partner? GI Joe underwear? Boy, you look *sharp*!"

Same thing with pajamas when you're three. You come downstairs at bedtime decked out in a snazzy pair of Barbie jammies, people will make such a fuss you'd think Princess Di walked in the room.

Now I'll tell you the best thing about being three: You don't have to carry any money. Everything is basically on the house.

When your family stops at Burger King, nobody expects you to whip out a twenty and announce: "Here, lemme get the Whoppers and fries."

Or say you're in the drugstore and suddenly you

get a craving for M&M's — you just grab those babies and bring them to the counter. Then you look at your mom or dad and it's an unspoken message: Pay the man.

It's even better than having a credit card. Because at the end of the month, when you've rung up a candy tab of, oh, two bucks, you're not sitting bleary-eyed at the kitchen table with a pile of bills in front of you and moaning: *"Tell me something, Doris! How are we gonna pay for this stuff?!"*

The simplest things excite people when you're three. Such as when you finish your peas at dinner.

If you finish your peas, people will gush: "Oh, honey, that's terrific! You're the best little boy in the whole world!"

It's unbelievable. They'll carry on like you just whipped global warming. And all you did was *finish your stupid peas*!

Meanwhile some poor scientist puts the finishing touches on the space probe to Pluto and people yawn and say: "Yeah, yeah, Pluto . . . who's on *Monday Night Football*?"

It's the same thing with artwork when you're three. No matter what kind of goofy drawing you hand your mom or dad, even if it's a billy goat with eight legs, they'll say: "Oh, honey, that's terrific!"

Meanwhile, in your heart, you know it's a lousy drawing. I mean, you might not be the brightest kid in the world, but even *you* know billy goats don't have eight legs. And you're only three!

Still, if adults are going to treat you as if you're the

logical successor to Renoir for these junky drawings, where's the incentive to get better?

Me, I'd keep drawing a billy goat with eight legs until some adult wised up and said: "Kid, this stuff is trash. Goats don't have eight legs. Now get with the program!"

Which, believe me, will never happen.

Adults don't have the guts to say that to a three-year-old.

Impressionism vs. post-modernism: Is it a tree or Baby Jesus?

The Artist, who just turned five, enters the room with a piece of construction paper on which is depicted a tableau of great emotional energy: jagged lines, bold circles, vivid splotches, all in various tasteful shades of crayon.

"It's . . . well, the only word is breathtaking," I say.

"Know what it is?" she asks.

"Of course," I say. "It's *life*. Feelings. Exhilaration. Confusion. The beastly fear that lurks in all of us — unless it's a tree."

"It's Baby Jesus," she says. "See, He's in the manger and here are Mary and Joseph. And these are the sheep."

"I knew that," I said. "The Christmas Story. The promise of God. A tiny Babe to live among men."

"And this," she says, "is the shining star that the Three Wise Men followed."

"A powerful piece of work," I say. "Spare, yet unrelenting. I don't know how you do it."

The Artist seems enormously proud of herself at this moment. Wordlessly, she hands me her latest work and we march solemnly into the kitchen and over to the refrigerator.

Then we secure four fruit magnets — two pineapples, a banana, and an orange, in this case —

and this newest creation is hung on the Sears Coldspot for all to admire.

That is the singular beauty of a young child's artwork: It is open to vast interpretation.

Certainly, it's rich in symbolism. Four squiggly brown lines, for instance, might represent a tree. Or they might be . . . Baby Jesus. In a manger. With, um, Mary and Joseph nearby.

In any event, there is a certain protocol to be observed when your child hands you his or her drawing and stands there patiently waiting for your reaction.

Perhaps the safest initial reaction a parent can have is: "Hmmmm . . ."

This vague response hints that you have been overwhelmed at the sheer brilliance and texture of the drawing, as well as the enormity of its theme.

More importantly, it buys you time to carefully inspect the drawing from all angles in order to determine exactly what the heck it's supposed to depict.

Turn the drawing upside down if you have to — that is, if you can figure out what upside down *is* in this case.

Then allow a soft smile of recognition to play across your features as you intone: "It's . . . it's beautiful!"

(Some parents like to embellish this scene by dabbing at their eyes with a handkerchief, as if overcome by the weighty realization that they are in the presence of the next Picasso or Georgia O'Keeffe. Personally, I find this to be a bit much. But if it works for you, go with it.)

The one thing you should never, ever say when a

child hands you a drawing is: "Oh, sweetie, it's . . . uh, what *is* it?"

Understand, it's not that this will hurt the child's feelings in any way.

Rather, your own feelings will be bruised when he or she stares at you as if you were a dunce and says (in an exasperated voice): "Silly . . . it's a Christmas tree with an angel on top!"

Right. The point is, it's always best to let the child volunteer any information concerning just what the theme of the artwork is supposed to be.

Because your guess, no matter how educated, will undoubtedly be wrong anyway. Also, just because a splotch of green and a yellow circle was a Christmas tree and angel in yesterday's drawing, it does not necessarily follow that they represent a tree and angel today.

Might be a sailboat, for all you know. Or a pussycat. It's all a crapshoot. So I would keep my mouth shut and let the child explain the drawing.

In the often esoteric world of child art, it is also considered bad form to point out, for example, that a sheep (such as, oh, the sheep in the drawing with Baby Jesus) does not have six legs.

Sifted through a child's imagination, a sheep apparently has . . . I don't know . . . as many legs as the child wants.

Accuracy of depiction and adherence to a reasonable measurement scale (Baby Jesus appeared to be some fifty feet tall, in this case) are not high priorities with very young artists.

To the young artist, depicting Baby Jesus as being

roughly the same size as a three-story building is perfectly okay.

Sure, the critics will rip that kind of haphazard rendering a few years down the line.

But you cross that bridge when you come to it.

Honesty is the best . . .
never mind

As an example of the moral degeneracy gripping the country, I offer this ugly little incident that occurred the other day.

The eleven-year-old and I were taking a walk in our neighborhood when we both spotted a twenty-dollar bill on the sidewalk.

Naturally, the boy lunged for the money, but I managed to trip him and slow him down.

He was up instantly and elbowed me in the gut, but I tackled him and the two of us tumbled to the sidewalk.

Nevertheless, he's a very strong boy and surprisingly agile for his size, and he managed to pounce on the bill first.

Then he held it up triumphantly.

Since the money was now in his hands and not mine, this seemed like a good time to teach him a lesson about honesty and responsibility.

"Son," I said, "by all rights, that twenty should be mine. I saw it first. Fair is fair. By the way, sorry about the tripping and tackling back there."

But the boy, who can be very hardheaded about these things, refused to hand over the money. Instead, he began blabbering something about possession being nine tenths of the law.

This, if you ask me, is the whole problem with the educational system in this country.

Instead of teaching reading and writing and basic

welding techniques for metal shop, as they did in my day, the schools now apparently try to ram pre-law courses down the students' throats.

The result is the unnerving sight of an eleven-year-old spouting legal maxims to his dad, who might as well have a small river of drool running down his chin for all he knows about basic property law.

Anyway, the boy was very pleased with himself and ran home to show his mother the money he'd found.

Of course, the sight of him so happy made me instantly depressed.

It's bad enough to see happy people in the best of circumstances. But to see someone who is deliriously happy when you're not is almost too much to bear.

Anyway, as soon as I got home, I delivered a second lecture to the boy about honesty and responsibility — this one even more stirring and heartfelt than the one before.

"Look," I said, "you should make an effort to see if any of the neighbors lost that money. How would *you* feel if you lost twenty bucks?"

Frankly, the boy did not seem terribly impressed with this suggestion, perhaps since it came from someone who had tried to maim him a few minutes earlier.

But he's a good boy, and he went off dutifully to knock on the doors of our neighbors.

As soon as he left, I jumped in the car and drove to the library at about seventy-five miles per hour, which I don't admit to proudly.

There I began rummaging through stacks of

lawbooks, finally finding what I was looking for in something known as *Black's Law Dictionary*.

Under a heading entitled "Replevin Action," it said: "An action whereby the owner or person entitled to repossession of goods or chattels may recover those goods or chattels from one who has wrongfully distrained or taken, or who wrongfully detains, such goods or chattels."

Of course, I had no idea what that meant. But it sounded impressive. More importantly, it contained a lot of big words that would surely confuse the boy and impress upon him the importance of handing over the money to me.

As you can imagine, I left the library in a fine mood. But the mood dissipated the moment I arrived home and found the boy was now being counseled by his mother.

The two informed me that none of the neighbors had reported losing twenty dollars.

Then my wife, who feels compelled to involve herself in *every* little thing that goes on around the house, to an astonishingly annoying degree, said: "And he's not giving *you* the twenty, either."

"Oh?" I said, pausing for dramatic effect. "Tell me, counselor, are you and your client familiar with the term 'replevin action'?"

Just as I figured, neither of them had heard the term before.

Unfortunately, neither one seemed to *care* what a replevin action was, either, with my wife adding: "You know what you can do with your replevin action, mister."

The boy said he was putting the twenty dollars toward a new pair of Rollerblades.

"You know, when I was your age, we didn't even *have* Rollerblades," I said. "We skated with, I don't know, old shoes that had bottle caps glued to the bottom for wheels!"

"You couldn't have had it *too* rough," the boy said. "Grandma said you had a big color TV growing up."

Forget the twenty bucks — *this* is another problem with the country: kids who don't even *pretend* to be impressed with the ridiculous tales you tell them.

Please. Don't get me started.

It beats a spike through your cheek

If memory serves, I had just drifted off for a nap, maybe even entered the all-important REM phase, when the twelve-year-old asked if we could talk about the "earring thing" again.

The gist of his argument was this: Earrings are cool and all his friends wear earrings, not to mention just about every guy in his school, and he'd like to wear one, too, except he can't because his old man is a fascist geek.

He didn't actually use the term "fascist geek," but that's probably what he was thinking.

"Look," I said, "if your mother and I let you wear an earring, you'll want a tattoo next, something with a big skull and flying dragons. And then you'll join an outlaw motorcycle gang and take up with a wild woman named Louise who'll talk you into holding up a bank or convenience store, for which you'll get caught and do hard time while Louise takes up with your best friend, Elmo.

"*That's* what an earring can lead to. You ask me, it's just not worth it."

He walked away shaking his head, and I sure couldn't blame him. It sounded like a lot of nonsense to me, too, but it was the best nonsense I could come up with on the spur of the moment.

That's the thing about kids: They're always asking you for something without giving you time to make up a good story. After a while, it *really* gets annoying.

Actually, I don't really have a problem with my son wearing an earring, if that's what he wants to do when he's a little older.

The fact is, I thought about getting an earring myself many years ago, except that I had a condition that prevented me from getting one, the condition being that I was too chicken.

This condition first surfaced the time me and Jim Cuso decided to get our ears pierced.

We ended up in this "head shop" — look, this was back in 1970, everyone was terminally stupid — where a man with long, stringy hair and maybe three teeth gave us each an ice cube to numb our earlobes.

Jim volunteered to go first, which was fine with me. In fact, I may have even pushed him into the chair.

Then the man pulled out a needle the size of a harpoon and jabbed Jim in the earlobe. Jim, the toughest linebacker on the school's football team, did not handle this well, unless you think screaming and carrying on is a good way to handle having your ear pierced.

"Well, forget *this*," I thought as I watched Jim. "Maybe I'll just get a nice paisley shirt instead."

So I never got my ear pierced and neither did Jim, for that matter. He freaked out so much that the head-shop owner gave us our money back and told us to get out.

The point is, I am certainly not anti-earring, although I favor tasteful studs or small hoops for men — not those big, dangly things that look like something Lola Falana wears on stage at the Sahara.

If you're a guy and you show up for work on the

loading dock with an earring like that, I'm sorry, people are going to talk.

The fact is, compared to some things kids are wearing these days, a guy with an earring is no big deal anymore.

Are you kidding? If you're a parent, your kid might come to you now and say: "I'm thinking of getting a nose ring, maybe something with five holes through both nostrils. Unless you think that's too *busy*?"

Or he could suddenly show up at the breakfast table with a six-inch silver spike implanted through his cheek. And when you say: "I, uh, can't help noticing that you have what appears to be a ten-penny nail sticking out of your face," he might answer: "Oh, this? Yeah, guy down at Bob's Body Surgery drove it through my cheek with a mallet last night. Pretty cool, huh?"

So an earring is no big deal. Heck, when my kid asks me for an earring, I'm almost tempted to reach in my pocket and say: "Sure, sure, here's a few bucks — get yourself three or four earrings. See if any of your friends want earrings, too. But, hey, young man: no spikes through the cheek, you hear me?"

Anyway, I think most guys with earrings look okay, with one obvious exception: old guys.

I remember when Ed Bradley of *60 Minutes* wore an earring. It just didn't look right. Ed looked like somebody's grandfather trying just a little too hard to be hip.

He'd be interviewing someone like Yasser Arafat, and you could see Arafat was sort of staring at Ed Bradley and thinking: "What's with the old dude and the earring? Wait'll I tell the boys back in Tunis about this."

Of course, times have changed. Now Ed Bradley could probably interview the Pope on network television with an eyebrow ring.

Especially if it was a small, tasteful eyebrow ring.

PART 6

♥

HOLIDAYS AND HOLY DAZE

Way beyond cool

The first thing you should know is that no one takes more pride in being a Catholic than I do, so let's not hear any nonsense to the contrary.

Still, the fact remains that being a Catholic on Ash Wednesday means looking like someone just tapped a cigarette out on your forehead. And hard as it is to believe, that kind of look is not considered cool by a lot of kids today.

Of course, it wasn't considered cool when I was a kid, either.

I remember my mother taking us for ashes at Sacred Heart Church back when my sister and I were in junior high school.

Me, I loved getting ashes. I loved the smell of the church that day. And I loved the crinkly feel of the ashes against my forehead, even when Father McCallen was handing them out.

Father McCallen had the touch of a blacksmith. He'd hit your forehead with his thumb and your head would snap back like you just took a straight right from George Foreman.

But as soon as we left the church, before the kids from the neighborhood could see us, my sister and I would rub off as much of the ashes as possible, although not enough to ruin whatever blessed charms they possessed.

See, to hear my mother tell it, the ashes would protect you from just about anything.

She was never very specific about this. But I had

the feeling that as long as you had ashes, you could pretty much walk in front of a runaway milk truck and walk away without a scratch.

Mom was born and raised in Ireland, and she also implied that ashes made you a little more special than everyone else.

Hearing this, I was always tempted to saunter into a candy store and start filling my pockets with candy. And if the guy behind the cash register gave me a hard time about paying for it, I'd say: "Friend, apparently you didn't see this mark on my forehead . . ."

Still, as much as we loved getting ashes, we'd cringe when kids who weren't Catholic sang out: "Hey, you been cleaning chimneys again? You got dirt on your forehead!"

That might sound terribly self-conscious to an adult. But you have to think back to when you were a kid. You have to remember how a twelve-year-old's mind works.

Take the most jittery, paranoid, unsure person you know and multiply that by a hundred, and that's basically the mind-set of your average twelve-year-old.

A twelve-year-old just wants to fit in. A twelve-year-old gets a pimple on his forehead and becomes convinced that everyone in the world is staring at it. A twelve-year-old is persuaded by his mom to wear a shirt his aunt got him for Christmas and spends the school day thinking: "They're all laughing at me in this dorky shirt."

So you have to expect at least a *little* anxiety when you all but say to a twelve-year-old: "Look, kid, here's the deal. We're gonna put a huge smudge of ashes on your forehead, and you have to walk around like that all day while some people stare and make comments."

For some twelve-year-olds, that's enough to make them lock themselves in a hall closet.

Anyway, now that I'm a parent of two near-adolescents, I have my own way of dealing with the self-consciousness that ashes can inspire.

On the way to church on Ash Wednesday, I remind the kids that we're not doing this just because we get a kick out of walking around with soot on our foreheads.

I remind them that this is the first day of Lent, the season of discipline and penitence.

I remind them that the ashes we're about to receive are from burned palms, and have been blessed by a priest.

I remind them that this blessing is based on the biblical passage ". . . for dust thou art, and unto dust thou shalt return."

And as soon as we leave the church, I tell them: "You guys look pretty cool with your ashes."

They don't believe me, of course. And as soon as we're in the car, they start rubbing the ashes off as I watch in the rearview mirror.

But I look on the bright side: I'm not twelve, so it's not *my* problem anymore.

Don't make me do it

For the Catholic parent of young children, Lent is a difficult time, especially if you have the sort of willpower that cracks like bone china.

Last year, for example, I decided to give up sweets for Lent.

To my wife and others who know me well, this was considered a supreme sacrifice.

Because this is the sort of person I am: If you and I happened upon a stray Hershey Kiss that had rolled under the couch months ago, and now it was all covered with dust and cobwebs and cat hair, and you made a move for it, I would grab you by the throat.

In other words, I have a bit of a sweet tooth. I say this with no great pride, either, because as a kid I had so many cavities, they set up a cot for me in the dentist's office.

Not too many kids sleep at the dentist's office, but I did. I was there so much, it felt like home. After a while, you don't even hear the drilling.

Anyway, I gave up sweets for Lent and was feeling enormously proud of myself — and certain that God was enormously proud of me, too — and this feeling of enormous pride lasted, oh, five minutes.

Which was when my oldest son, who was ten at the time, sat next to me with a plate of Oreos.

For the record, Oreos are the best cookies in the world, and if you don't think so, you should probably have your head examined. Really.

This is how much I like Oreos: If you and I

happened upon the last Oreo in the cookie jar, and it was moldy and cracked and half the filling was missing, and you made a move for it, I would bite your hand.

You think I'm kidding, but I'm not. I bit my wife's hand once when she reached for one of my Oreos. We were at the neighbors' house at the time. As you can imagine, it caused a bit of a scene.

Later, when we got home, my wife said: "You shouldn't have done that in front of Janet and Rich."

And I said: "The way Rich was eyeing my Oreos, I was gonna bite him, too."

Anyway, my son sat down with his Oreos, which sort of got my attention, the way a can of spinach gets Popeye's attention, if you catch my drift.

"Hi! What's going on?" he said.

At first I didn't answer him, as I was lost in thought, trying to figure out what I was going to do if he made a move for one of those cookies.

Finally I said: "Did you know I gave up sweets for Lent?"

"Oh," he said at first, and then *"Ohhh!"* as the lightbulb came on over his head. Then he quickly grabbed the Oreos and left the room, which was a good thing. Ain't no flies on that boy, as the old saying goes.

Once again I was feeling enormously proud of myself. And this time the feeling of pride lasted maybe ten minutes, until my daughter, who was eight, sat next to me with a dish of Breyer's chocolate ice cream.

Any fool knows that Breyer's chocolate ice cream is the greatest ice cream ever made. And if you don't agree with that, I suggest you get the Yellow Pages out right now and look under "Psychiatrists and Psychologists." Because you need one.

This is how much I love Breyer's chocolate ice cream: If you and I happened to pull a carton out of the freezer and there was only, like, a couple of spoonfuls left, mostly melted stuff that was fused into the cardboard, and you made a move for it, I would stomp on your foot real hard. And if that didn't stop you, I would slam the freezer door on your hand — without hesitation.

So here was my daughter sitting there with a bowl of this great ice cream. And as she picked up her spoon, I decided to say something, for her sake.

"Don't do it," I whispered.

She looked puzzled, so I whispered again: "Remember Daddy gave up sweets for Lent?"

Well, the girl is no fool. She took her ice cream and left the room in a hurry, shooting worried looks over her shoulder, the way you would if some strange person was talking to himself behind you.

Anyway, to make a long story short, I didn't crack and went the entire period of Lent last year without any sweets. And I didn't kill anyone, either, if that's what you're thinking.

This Lent, I decided to give up beer. I better *not* see anyone wandering around the house with a Heineken.

Because let me tell you: If you and I were at a cookout and there was only one Heineken left in the cooler, and it was sort of dirty-looking and had leaves and grass sticking to it, and you made a move for it, you'd be in big trouble.

More than a man can stand

Let me say that I'm not one of these people who talks about how selfish the younger generation is, although that policy might have to be revised in light of certain recent developments.

I speak here of a nasty incident with a chocolate bunny that has both unnerved me and cast a pall of mistrust and bitterness over my wife and children.

The chocolate bunny was, of course, a by-product of Easter and that peculiar tradition whereby Catholic parents patiently explain to their kids about the death and resurrection of Jesus Christ — only to then veer off into a bizarre tale of some giant philanthropic rabbit who will be bringing them candy.

This alone would get a child all wound up, of course. But then after Mass on Easter Sunday, we sit idly by and watch as the kids ingest massive amounts of chocolate into their system.

The net result (at least with my kids) is that they spend the day speeding around the house like deranged road runners until collapsing limp and exhausted at, oh, one in the morning.

Anyway, with all the other cavity-producing loot the kids raked in this Easter, they paid little or no attention to this chocolate bunny I mentioned earlier.

It sat there all by itself on the kitchen counter, wrapped in clear plastic and sporting a perky smile on its face.

For two days, no one touched this chocolate bunny. In fact, I myself barely gave it a glance, exercising the kind of self-control found only in isolated Tibetan monasteries and, perhaps, in Jane Fonda.

Then on the third day, I cracked.

Oh, I cracked big time. And I attacked this chocolate bunny with a savagery that was truly alarming to see in a forty-three-year-old man.

Thankfully, there was no one home during the assault, which came while I was laboring over a particularly wretched column.

My line of reasoning is a little unclear at this point. But apparently I thought that a piece of chocolate would serve as a much-needed jolt to my central nervous system.

And this, I hoped, would stimulate my creative juices and lift the column from the ranks of the particularly wretched to the normal state of wretchedness my readers have come to expect.

With this in mind, then, I unwrapped the chocolate bunny. And then I . . . well, God help me, but I tore his little ear off his head! And I ate it.

Boy, it tasted great. In fact, it tasted so great that I tore off the bunny's other little ear and ate that, too. Then I went to work on his head, arms, and upper torso before finishing him off one leg at a time.

Then I went back to my column, which, despite the chocolate rush, nevertheless ended up being particularly wretched. Of course, this only hastens the day when I quit writing professionally and open a small deli and spend my day making cold cut subs for beefy construction workers.

Anyway, that evening, as I lay on the couch

studying the ceiling, a loud mournful wailing erupted from the kitchen.

This was followed by the sound of hurried footsteps and a young voice crying out: *"Someone ate the bunny!"*

Naturally, I did what any other father would do in this situation, which was to grab my coat and car keys and beat it out the back door.

Then I gunned the car in the direction of the mall, where I spent the next two hours in front of a Hickory Farms store, staring at a disturbing assortment of smoked sausage and wondering where my life had gone wrong.

Unfortunately, the heat was still on when I returned home. As soon as I walked in the door, people were shooting me dirty looks, as if I'd dragged in a corpse behind me.

Finally, my wife gave me a withering look and said: "Are you the pathetic, twisted individual who ate that chocolate bunny?"

Well. I'll tell you something about a question like that. Right away it puts you on the defensive.

My first instinct, honed by years of experience in such matters, was, of course, to lie.

But the more I thought about it . . . hey, what exactly were we going to do with that chocolate bunny, anyhow? Use him as a doorstop? Or a paperweight?

Nobody was eating him, right? So that stupid chocolate bunny would have sat around the house for weeks, drawing ants and spiders and maybe even eventually gangs of marauding mice.

The way I looked at it, I'd just saved us a thousand bucks or more in exterminator fees.

"Heck, yes!" I said at last. "I ate that bunny! You want details? I ate his little ears first and then his head and his arms. His little legs were the best, though, nice and crunchy. *And now he's all gone! Do you hear me? Gone! Ha, ha, ha!*"

I don't remember what happened next, except my wife and kids were staring at me wide-eyed, and then everyone just sort of drifted away.

I'll tell you something: Honesty is not all it's cracked up to be.

Although it's nice and quiet around the house right now.

Midnight Mass madness

One Christmas Eve a few years ago, my two older kids, seven and four at the time, begged me to take them to Midnight Mass. Apparently a large piano had recently fallen on my head from a great height, because I said yes.

The kids took a long nap in the afternoon to prepare for the experience. My wife wasn't joining us that evening — she was staying home to "help" Santa. So I spent several hours while the kids were resting combing through various medical texts to discover what sort of synaptical brain malfunction had occurred that a father would agree to such a venture on his own.

Here is a chronicle of the events, as best as can be recalled:

▲ **Midnight** — The children are terribly excited. Midnight Mass! And Santa's coming after that! The seven-year-old's legs are jiggling like he just slammed back six cups of Folgers. The four-year-old is rocking back and forth, back and forth, back and forth in her seat — I'm afraid she might actually begin levitating toward the ceiling.

▲ **12:02 A.M.** — It suddenly occurs to me that we're sitting just four rows from the altar, which might be a huge mistake, given the emotional state of these kids.

I just hope this isn't one of those wimpy priests who gets all rattled every time some kid shoots to her feet and cries out something about Santa bringing her a Malibu Beach Barbie.

A priest who was in 'Nam during the Tet Offensive, that's what we need now.

▲ **12:03** — Well, that didn't take long. In a whisper loud enough to be heard in the next county, the four-year-old asks when Mass will be over.

She also wants to know if Santa has delivered her presents yet. I tell her that Santa always waits until children are home and fast asleep in their beds before delivering their presents and that he, um, *personally* assured me that this policy never varies.

She doesn't seem convinced. Of course, after hearing a story that lame, I don't blame her.

▲ **12:07** — We made it to the first reading, but the seven-year-old's fidgeting has increased markedly in intensity. His feet are jiggling up and down like twin pistons, creating a *womp, womp, womp* noise as they bang against the kneeler. The woman in front of us turns and shoots me a dirty look.

Maybe this is why they have two readings — in case you miss the first one because of some wired little kid banging away behind you.

▲ **12:10** — The seven-year-old asks in a low voice if I think Santa will bring him Super Nintendo, which he asked the Santa at the mall for, although not the Santa that came to visit his school or the Santa at the Christmas fair.

I'm so confused, I ask if he can please put the question in writing, so I can diagram all the Santas.

▲ **12:15** — Uh-oh, we made it to the homily, but the first signs of anarchy are becoming visible. The seven-year-old just snatched a songbook from the four-year-old, who grabbed him by the shirt. I remind both children that we are in God's House and that Santa only brings presents to good little boys and girls.

With that, the two smile at each other angelically and fold their hands neatly in their laps. I feel like taking a Polaroid snapshot and bringing it home to my wife so we can play "What's Wrong With This Picture?"

▲ **12:27** — Grabbing my shoulder excitedly, the four-year-old whispers that she's spotted Rudolph the Red-Nosed Reindeer in the Nativity scene behind us.

No, I tell her, that's a lamb, which you can tell by its lamblike wool, its lamblike face, legs, and tail, and by the fact that every other part of it looks like a lamb, too.

Briefly, I worry about the child's academic future if she can't even tell a lamb from a reindeer, but I attribute the mix-up to an overdose of Christmas Eve excitement.

Although we might want to have her eyes checked, pronto.

▲ **12:28** — Looking to head off the next question, I assure the four-year-old that that's Baby Jesus in the manger, not Baby Santa.

▲ **12:37** — The four-year-old grabs my ear, pulls me toward her, and wants to know how Santa gets all the toys for all the good little boys and girls in the whole world into that one tiny sleigh.

Rather than get into a long, convoluted explanation about packing techniques, space-distribution theories, and weight-transference ratios, I whisper: "He just *does*. Now turn around."

This is what happens when: (a) you don't know the

answer, and (b) half your ear has been pulled from its mooring.

My nerves are strung tighter than piano wire.

▲ **12:45** — Time for Communion. The situation in Row 4 is deteriorating rapidly. Sure, there are other pockets of restless kids throughout the church. But our row is like the exercise yard at San Quentin. It could blow at any moment.

▲ **12:57** — Closing hymn already? Gee, where does the time go? I ask the kids if they'd like to look at the Nativity scene before we leave, even though I realize it's not as compelling without, ahem, Rudolph.

But the kids are already halfway to the parking lot. I take it that means "no."